NAKED GENIUS

Copyright © 1982 by
The Chapel Hill Historical Society
Manufactured in the United States of America
Printed by the Greensboro Printing Company, Greensboro, North Carolina

Library of Congress Catalog Card No. 82-71039

ISBN 978-1-7338540-4-7

Reprinted April 2022

Cover Image: University of North Carolina Campus, 1855

NAKED GENIUS

By

George Moses Horton

The Colored Bard of North Carolina

A publication of

To make available to present and future generations those works that will enrich the perception of Chapel Hill and its environs, preserve those aspects of its heritage that can be compressed between covers, and sustain the traditions for which the village and its people have so long been known.

*"I commend you and the Society for your plans to publish a facsimile of George Moses Horton's "Naked Genius." We would all gain from it — **will** all gain from it."*

— Paul Green
January 26, 1981

Previous Publications of
the Chapel Hill Historical Society

These Old Stone Walls
by Phillips Russell
1972

Historic Buildings and Landmarks of Chapel Hill
1973, 1975

When Chapel Hill was a Village
by Cornelia Spencer Love
1976

The Oral History of James Nunn,
by W. Wilder Towle
1977

Growing Up With Chapel Hill
by Jane Toy Coolidge
1977

1818 Pictorial Map
1976

Calendars
1978, 1979, 1980, 1981

This book is fondly dedicated to John Macfie, who served for so long and with such dedication as Chairman of the Publications Committee of The Chapel Hill Historical Society.

The Society regrets that illness forced John Macfie's resignation as Chairman before the publication of this facsimile of George Moses Horton's *Naked Genius* could be completed, and that he is not here with us now to enjoy the completion of this project. Yet it is his, nonetheless.

Acknowledgments

The Chapel Hill Historical Society and its Publications Committee wish to express appreciation to the Library of The Boston Athenaeum and to its Director and Librarian, Rodney Armstrong, for the cooperation extended in publishing this facsimile copy of *Naked Genius* from the original manuscript in the Confederate Imprints collection at The Boston Athenaeum.

The Society is indebted to Richard Walser for his kindness and generosity in writing the biographical sketch of George Moses Horton that appears in this book, drawn from material he used in his biography of Horton, *The Black Poet*.

The Society wishes to thank Didi Dunphey, artist illustrator, for her generosity and kindness in providing the drawing that illustrates this edition, and for her guidance on artistic matters concerned with its publication.

The Society also wishes to thank the members of the Publications Committee for their time and dedication to this project — Mrs. Wayne Bowers; Mr. David J. Brunn, Mr. Jerry W. Cotten, Mrs. Didi Dunphey, Dr. Douglas J. Eyre, Mrs. Leo Gardiner, Mr. Wallace H. Kuralt, Jr., Mr. J. Maryon (Spike) Saunders, Dr. Ralph M. Watkins, Mr. Clarence Whitefield, and Miss Val Lauder, Chairman.

Introduction

Naked Genius is one of the rarest titles in Americana. It was the third book of a recently freed slave, published in Raleigh the latter part of 1865 by William B. Smith, printer in the town, and almost immediately forgotten. Nowadays, however, if a copy should turn up at an auction, it would fetch an impressive sum.

* * *

"I was born in Northampton County, N.C., near the line of Virginia, and within four miles of the Roanoke River," wrote George Moses Horton in 1845, "the property of William Horton, senior, who also owned my mother, and the whole stock of her children, which were five before me, all girls, but not of one father. I am the oldest child that my mother had by her second husband, and she had four younger than myself, one boy and three girls. But to account for my age is beyond the reach of my power." Most researchers have concluded that he was born about 1797.

At the turn of the century, William Horton and several of his six sons left their worn-out tobacco plantations in Northampton and moved inland to Chatham County, where the soil was more fertile. They bought land between the Haw River and New Hope Creek, nine miles from the courthouse at Pittsboro and eight miles from the university village of Chapel Hill. Thereafter, for ten years, reported the young slave, he became a "bow-boy" attending his master's cattle. It was during this time that he became "fond of hearing people read" and yearned to acquire the ability himself. He got hold of some old spelling books, taught himself to identify the letters, and went "in the summer season to some shady and lonely recess... [to] stammer over the dim and promiscuous syllables." At night, he studied by the flickering light coming from the oak logs on the hearth, becoming "almost exhausted by the heat of the fire and almost suffocated with smoke." Only his mother and younger brother were aware of what he was doing.

Poetry was his favorite reading material, and whenever he noticed structured lines in some discarded paper, he pored over the words in great excitement. The only books available to him were the New Testament and a copy of Charles Wesley's hymns. His first poem came "one very calm Sabbath morning" and went like this:

> Rise up, my soul, and let us go
> Up to the gospel feast;
> Gird on the garment white as snow,
> To join and be a guest.

Since he could not write, the words were "memorized" and kept in his head.

In 1814, William gave his tall, handsome chattel to son James, and a few years later the slave was allowed to go to Chapel Hill on Sundays to sell farm produce to the students there. The hundred or so "scholars" at the University of North Carolina spent most of their time composing orations to be delivered at meetings of the literary societies. From the slaves who dispensed vegetables and fruit, the prankish young gentlemen often demanded that they "spout" an oration before a sale was completed. George Moses was inept at oratory, but when he substituted a poem that he declared was his own, the students were incredulous. As a test, they provided him with a girl's name on which to write an acrostic. During the following week he worked at the crucial experiment, and on Sunday walked off to Chapel Hill, his brain rhythmically swaying with the words of the required acrostic, which he said had been "composed at the handle of the plough." A student copied down the lines as he recited them.

Before long the students commissioned Horton to write acrostics to send to their sweethearts back home. Tradition persists that James Knox Polk, class of 1818 and later President of the United States, was the first to encourage Horton, but according to the slave it was Augustus Alston of Georgia who "first laid (as he said) the low price of twenty-five cents on my compositions each . . . but some gentlemen, extremely generous, have given me from fifty to seventy-five cents." With Alston's twenty-five cents paid and received, Horton became the first black professional writer in America. For the rest of his life, he supported himself, at least partially, from his fees.

In 1826, the Massachusetts novelist and poet Caroline Lee Hentz, wife of the esteemed French arachnologist Nicholas Marcellus Hentz, arrived in Chapel Hill. She taught her black friend how to improve his poems and began helping him learn to write. To her hometown newspaper back in Massachusetts she sent several of his poems, and in the *Lancaster Gazette* on April 8, 1828, "Liberty and Slavery," Horton's introduction to print, appeared.

That very summer, Professor and Mrs. Hentz teamed up with liberal editor Joseph Gales of the *Raleigh Register* and his wife the novelist Winifred Marshall Gales to plan purchasing Horton's freedom and providing him transportation to Liberia. Horton was happy at the prospect, perhaps anticipating an election to the office of Poet Laureate of Liberia. The American Colonization Society was alerted, the antislavery *Freedom's Journal* in New York City fanned the campaign, and the violent black abolitionist David C. Walker of Boston made a pledge of hard cash. In North Carolina, the Hentz and Gales families were joined by none other than Governor John Owen, who the slave said proposed to James Horton "to pay $100 more than any person of sound judgment should say that I was worth." To raise more money still, Joseph Gales in 1829 published a little pamphlet of Horton's poems titled *The Hope of Liberty*, most of the selections bemoaning his status as a slave. This slight little publication has the distinction of being the first book by a Negro in the South. With it, Horton became the third black person in America to write a book, only Jupiter Hammon and Phillis Wheatley having preceded him.

Dr. James Henderson, the village physician, and University President Joseph Caldwell were among those who hoped for the success of the campaign, but *The Hope of Liberty* attracted few purchasers, money from the North failed to arrive, and soon the effort to purchase Horton subsided. It seems, furthermore, that Master James Horton had no intention of selling George Moses at any figure.

During the 1830s, George Moses managed to "hire out his time" by paying James Horton twenty-five cents a day to keep from working on the farm. He rambled about Chapel Hill, frequented the dormitories and the campus haunts, and was able to secure commissions for twenty or so poems a week, most of them mere rhyming nonsense with which the students were enchanted. Horton was distressed in 1835 when President Caldwell died. Caldwell not only had lent him many books to read but was a powerful ally when support was needed. The new president, ex-Governor David L. Swain, was not so fascinated by the Sable Bard, as Horton came to be known.

In 1843, upon the death of James Horton, George Moses became the property of his son Hall Horton, who set a new amount of fifty cents a day for hiring out his time. This outrageous turn of events required the poet to devise some plan to increase his income. He put together a manuscript of poems, sought subscribers for its publication, and hoped the scheme would work. When *The Poetical Works of George M. Horton, the Colored Bard of North Carolina* was issued in 1845 by Dennis Heartt of Hillsborough, its ninety-nine Subscribers' Names included President Swain, Professor William Mercer Green, Chapel Hill's Mayor John H. Watson, and eighty-one students, among them Alfred Moore Scales, a future governor of North Carolina. This little volume of fewer than a hundred pages, introduced by an autobiographical sketch, sold for fifty cents, but seems not to have brought its author much revenue. Instead of the antislavery poems of his earlier book, *Poetical Works* catered to students' tastes in artificial lyrics that sacrificed content and meaning to jingling rhyme.

During these years, Horton continued to seek some means by which he could obtain his freedom. He wrote to William Lloyd Garrison, to Horace Greeley, and doubtless other prominent personages of the day. Unfortunately, he chose President Swain to forward these letters to the great men; the savvy university president, in the troubled political climate of North Carolina, had no intention of becoming an intermediary in such a matter as traffic in slaves. On two occasions, the Sable Bard went so far as to ask Swain to purchase him, citing Hall Horton's figure of $250, but the offer was politely declined. In the cotton-rich Southland of the 1850s, Horton lapsed into a reasonable content, pursuing his poetic calling among the 460 students at the university, second in size only to Yale among American colleges.

Nothing is known about how Horton idled his time in those calamitous years following Fort Sumter. From pages in *Naked Genius*, it seems that he continued to write poems, even when there were no paying customers, and that, finally, it occurred to him that indeed he might soon be set free of bondage. In April 1865, a unit of Sherman's victorious army was stationed in Chapel Hill to guard the village and university buildings. One of the captains of the 9th Michigan Cavalry Volunteers was Will H. S. Banks of Lawton, Michigan. Regardless of whether Horton approached Banks, or Banks approached Horton, the two met and projected a new book of poems. As editor, Banks looked over what Freedman Horton showed him but wanted to add a sizable group of new poems.

Always a rapid producer, Horton happily undertook the task. Banks later told how the Black Poet had been "hard at work both night and day composing poems for his new book and writing acrostics for the boys on their sweethearts' names." It was like the old days, except that Union soldiers now replaced university students. When the 9th Michigan left Chapel Hill, Horton went along westward with them to Greensboro, Lexington, and Concord. In mid-July, at which time the troops were mustered out, Banks and Horton moved on to Raleigh and secured William B. Smith, Republican printer, to set the manuscript in type. Fearing that this literary product by an ex-slave would be taken as a fake, Banks carefully listed those who would vouch for its integrity: President Swain, Judge William H. Battle, Hall Horton, and a battery of Federal officers. Though Banks had high hopes for *Naked Genius*, this third and last of Horton's titles was doomed to financial failure, like his first two. Banks's undertaking came to nothing.

After the printing of the book, editor and poet journeyed north, Banks to his home in Michigan, Horton to Philadelphia. For the old man, the big city fell short of expectations. During the next eighteen years, Horton eked out an existence writing for Sunday School publications and working in the households of North Carolina friends like the Cobb family. Not long before he died in 1883, Collier Cobb visited him in Philadelphia and called him "Poet," to which the ancient bard replied,

"That pleased me greatly, Professor Cobb... you are using my proper title."

* * *

Of the 132 poems in Naked Genius, 42 came from *Poetical Works*. To honor his new sponsors, Horton wrote on President Lincoln, on Union generals Grant and Sherman. There were patriotic poems, poems based on events in Lexington and Concord recently experienced, surrogate poems like "A Faint Description from the Plains of Michigan." Among the best ones are a few describing conditions in North Carolina immediately after the war. Yet the poems are remarkable mainly as evidence of the remarkable life and professional career of a black poet whose "genius" would not be denied.

— Richard Walser

Based on material from his biography *The Black Poet: Being the Remarkable Story of George Moses Horton, a North Carolina slave*.

NAKED GENIUS:

BY

GEORGE MOSES HORTON,

THE COLORED BARD OF NORTH CAROLINA,

AUTHOR OF "THE BLACK POET,"

A WORK BEING NOW COMPILED AND REVISED BY CAPTAIN WILL. H. S. BANKS, 9TH MICHIGAN CAVALRY VOLUNTEERS, AND WHICH WILL BE READY FOR PUBLICATION ABOUT THE 1ST OF OCTOBER, 1865. THIS WORK WILL CONTAIN A CONCISE HISTORY OF THE LIFE OF THE AUTHOR, WRITTEN BY THE COMPILER, AND WILL BE OFFERED TO THE PUBLIC AS ONE OF THE MANY PROOFS THAT GOD, IN HIS INFINITE WISDOM AND MERCY, CREATED THE BLACK MAN FOR A HIGHER AND NOBLER PURPOSE THAN TO TOIL HIS LIFE AWAY UNDER THE GALLING YOKE OF SLAVERY.

REVISED AND COMPILED BY

WILL. H. S. BANKS,

CAPT. 9TH MICH. CAV.

WM. B. SMITH & CO.:

SOUTHERN FIELD AND FIRESIDE BOOK PUBLISHING HOUSE,
RALEIGH, N. C.
1865.

COPY RIGHT APPLIED FOR ACCORDING TO LAW.

INTRODUCTION.

Having met with the author of these works during the victorious march of our army through the State of North Carolina, he having been one of the many refugees who flocked to our lines for safety, I was astonished at his genius, and more so when he showed me some manuscripts written by himself. Knowing the various objections which many of our citizens, north as well as south, have against the black man being made free, and one of these being that he possessed no genius, I formed the idea that I would revise and compile his works and have them published to the public at large, that all might see that there are erroneous opinions entertained with regard to African genius, and also to show that God in his gifts was in no wise partial to the Uuropean, but that he gave genius to the black as well as the white man. With this object in view, I offer this little volume to the public, hoping that it may do away with some of the many prejudices so long existing against the poor down-trodden sou'a of Africa. To those who doubt the author's genius, I offer the following references:

EX-GOV. DAVID L. SWAIN, Chapel Hill, N. C.
JUDGE BATTLE, Chapel Hill, N. C.
DENNIS HART, Editor Hillsboro' Recorder.
HALL HART, his late master, who is now a resident of Chatham Co. N. C.

The above named gentlemen have been personally acquainted with Mr. Horton for the last forty years, and can testify to the wonderful genius he possesses, which is purely void of the garb of education. To still further remove any doubts which might arise in the minds of the public as to his being the author of the following poetical effusions, I refer them to the under named officers of the regiment to which I belong, who are all knowing to the fact of my being engaged with Mr. Horton in collecting and revising his poems.

> GEO. S. ACKER, Colonel.
> W. B. WAY, Lieutenant-Colonel.
> S. P. BROCKWAY, Major.
> W. C. STEVENS, Major.
> JAS. C. McBRIDE, Major.
> WM. H. YOUNG, Surgeon.
> A. FLETCHER.
> L. F. JOHNSON, Captain Company A.
> JAS. J. LISTER, Captain Company B.
> J. D. SMAILS, 1st Lieutenant Company C.
> T. E. CAMBERN, 2d Lieutenant Company D.
> JNO J. HINCHEY, Captain Company E.
> A. B. HENDRICKS, Captain Company F.
> A HINES, Captain Company G.
> A. P. PIERSON, 1st Lieutenant Company H.
> G. E. TURNER, Captain Company I.
> L. F. LOCKWOOD, Captain Company K.
> D. P. INGRAHAM, Captain Company L.
> CHAS. H. SMITH, 1st Lieutenant Company M.

Very respectfully, your obedient servant,
WILL. H. S. BANKS,
Capt. Co. C., 9th Mich. Cav. Vols.

SKETCH OF THE AUTHOR.

GEORGE MOSES HORTON was born of slave parents in Northampton County, North Carolina, on the Roanoke river, the property of Wm Horton, Sen. To account for his exact age is beyond the reach of the compiler, as slaves seldom know their ages; but from the most reliable information which he has been able to gain from those who have been acquainted with the author from childhood up to the present time, he was probably born about the year 1794. In the course of five or six years after his birth, from the sterility of his land, his old master moved with his family into Chatham County, a more fertile and fresh part of the country recently settled, and whose waters were far more healthy and agreeable. Here, as a field hand on his master's plantation he spent his days, till 1815, at which time his master died, leaving him the property of his oldest son, James. It was about this time he commenced composing poetry, and being without a knowledge of the use of letters, he dictated while others reduced his poems to writing. In this way he produced many beautiful poems and hymns which were eagerly sought for, and not a few of them were published extensively in different papers throughout the State. He soon, however, formed the resolve to learn to read and write, and how far he succeeded will hereafter be seen. In 1832 his second master died, and he was put up at auction, and purchased, unfortunately for the author, by his late master's son, "Hall," who was a hard master, and denied him of every advantage which he might improve for the edification of his mind. But notwithstanding the accumulated difficulties which he had to surmount, he determined to study letters. Each Sabbath he would retire to some secluded spot and spend the day in looking over such old pieces of books as he could collect without exciting too strongly the suspicion of his master, who was ever ready and willing to chastise him for any attempt at learning. In the year 1840, he hired his time at twenty-five cents per day, and employed himself as a servant at the State University, located at Chapel Hill. Here, through the kindness of many of the students, he became a tolerable good reader and a passable writer, which gave him a far better chance to employ the wonderful powers he possessed. To the very distinguished Mrs. Hentz of Boston, the author owes much, for the correction of many poetical errors. Being a poetess herself, and a lover of genius, she discovered his uncultivated talent, and was moved by pity to uncover to him the beauties of correctness, together with the true object to which he aspired. This celebrated lady did not remain long at Chapel Hill, in 1843 she returned to her home in Massachusetts. The loss of a friend so kind and good was to Mr. Horton a severe blow; but, however much he felt the loss of her instructions, he continued writing, and in 1845 produced his first book, consisting of a series of miscellaneous poems, and published by Dennis Heart, Esq , Editor of the Hillsboro' Recorder. By this time the fame of the colored bard went with lightning speed wherever the prejudice of the people would permit his poems to go. Many of his books were sold in different parts of the State, and but for the fact of his being a slave, and the influence which a few of the leading men brought to bear against him, that precious gem of African genius would have found a ready place in the hands of one million of the people of the North. 'Tis true he had his friends and admirers, but where the laws of a State binds the African with fetters, a few private individuals can render him but little service. In 1832, Governor Owen, Doctor Caldwell and Doctor Henderson made propositions to his master for his purchase for the purpose of sending him to Liberia, but Mr. Horton saw a fortune in dat niggah, and wouldn't sell, unless he could get enough to buy about four good field hands. Such an exorbitant price these gentlemen were unwilling to pay, and abandoned their project. Having no other hopes of freedom, our author was doomed to remain in slavery—to toil without rest, under the unrelenting eye of his master, till the occupation of Raleigh by our troops, when he escaped to our lines for protection, and is now with the writer bard at work both night and day composing poems for his book, and writing acrostics for the boys on their sweethearts' names, in which he takes great delight.

THE COMPILER.

INDEX.

	PAGE
The Musical Chamber,	9
George Moses Horton, Myself,	10
A Dirge,	11
Death of a Favorite,	12
The Fearful Traveller in the Haunted Castle,	13
To Catherine,	15
The Swan—Vain Pleasures,	15
Gen. Grant—The Hero of the War,	16
The Powers of Love,	18
To a Departing Favorite,	19
Sherman the Great,	20
The Heroes of the Late War,	21
The Southern Refugee,	22
The Slave,	23
Fare Thee Well, But Not Forever,	24
The Traveller,	25
Recent Appearance of a Lady,	27
Meditations on a Cold, Dark and Rainy Night,	28
Gen. Kilpatrick, the Bold Cavalier,	29
Lincoln is Dead,	30
On an Old Deluded Suitor,	31
The Woodman and the Money Hunter,	32
The Eye of Love,	33
The Creditor to His Proud Debtor,	34
Pleasures of Hope,	35
A Slave's Reflections the Eve Before His Sale,	36
Farewell to Frances,	37
The Retreat from Moscow,	38
Imploring to be Resigned at Death,	40
The Graduate Leaving College,	41
To the King of Macedonia,	42
Division of an Estate,	43
Pride in Heaven,	44
To Miss Tempe,	46

INDEX.

	PAGE.
Man, A Torch,	46
Like Brothers We Meet,	47
The Dying Soldier's Message,	48
The Treacherous Woman,	49
The Spectator of the Battle of Belmont,	50
Liberty,	51
Execution of Private Henry Anderson,	51
A Dirge on the Same,	53
The Guilty Judge,	54
The Flag of the Free,	55
One Generation Passeth Away and Another Cometh,	56
A Visit to My Master's Grave,	57
Death of an Old Carriage Horse,	57
The Rising Sun,	58
The Setting Sun,	59
Memory,	60
Prosperity,	61
Death of Gen. Jackson—An Eulogy,	62
Mr. Clay's Reception at Raleigh,	63
Clay's Defeat,	65
Slavery,	66
The Terrors of War,	68
The Happy Bird's Nest,	69
The Fate of an Innocent Dog,	69
The Tippler to his Bottle,	72
Rosabella—Purity of Heart,	73
False Weight,	74
Departing Summer,	75
Reflections from the Flash of a Meteor,	76
True Friendship,	77
On the Conversion of a Sister,	78
Early Affection,	79
Connubial Felicity,	80
No, Never Love,	81
Discarded by a False Suitor,	82
Recollections of Past Events,	83
The Intemperance Club,	84
Jefferson in a Tight Place,	84
Gen. Jordan, &c.,	86
The Soldier on His Way Home,	87

	PAGE.
The Soldier at Home,	88
The Angel of Death at the Bed of a Dying Saint,	89
The Flight of Thought,	89
Poverty,	90
The Use of Liberty,	92
Eulogy on the Death of a Sister,	93
The late Thunder Storm while in Camp, &c.,	94
McCroom to His Miss,	96
Advice to the Extravagant, Proud and Idle,	96
The Art of a Poet,	98
The Mammoth,	99
Alexander the Great,	99
Regretted Past Time,	101
The Hermit's View from the Mountain,	102
Song of Liberty,	103
She Avered she knew not what to Sing,	104
The Eye Drop,	104
Touch Not, Handle Not, Taste Not,	106
To the Fourth—(July 4th, 1865,)	107
Hard is the Sentence of Parting Man and Wife, &c.,	109
A Wife, A Wife, A Wife, &c.,	110
Beware! I am Gone,	110
The Power of Love,	112
The Horse Stolen from the Camp,	113
Weep,	113
Negro Speculation,	114
The Pleasures of Free Grace, &c.,	115
The Cheerless Condition of Bachelorship,	116
The Thought of Home in Battle,	118
The Memory of a Lady in Battle,	119
The Friends Left at Home,	120
Davis' Flight,	122
After His Departure,	122
Farewell! Farewell!	124
Peace at Home,	125
My Native Home,	126
New Fashions,	127
Aspiring Home,	129
Freedom,	130
The Union of Parties,	132

INDEX.

	PAGE.
Song of Liberty and Parental Advice,	133
Sing On,	136
At Leaving Camp,	137
Languishing for Some One,	138
The Unawakened Penitent Returning from the Camp,	140
Snaps for Dinner, Snaps for Breakfast and Snaps for Supper,	142
To the Muse,	143
The Close of Life,	144
On Epiphany,	145
Rachael or Virtue,	146
The Soldier's Thought of Home at the End of the War,	147
A Faint Description from the Plains of Michigan,	148
From Leaving Home,	149
Let me be There,	150
A Beautiful Moonlight Night in April,	151
Assassination of Abrahæn Lincoln,	154
Mrs. Lincoln's Lamentations,	155
The Obstructions of Genius,	157

NAKED GENIUS.

THE MUSICAL CHAMBER.

I trust that my friends will remember,
    Whilst I these my pleasures display;
Resort to my musical chamber,
    The laurel crown'd desert in May.

Resort to this chamber at leisure,
    Attend it by night and by day;
To feast on the dainties of pleasure
    Which cannot be stinted in May.

This chamber is both pleasing and moral,
    A chamber both lov'ly and gay,
In the shade of a ne'er fading laurel,
    Whose grace in December is May.

Abounding with every fine story
    Whilst time passes hurrying away;
This place is a banquet of glory,
    Which rings with the ditties of May.

The chamber of Chatham and Dolly,
    A place of Comical play;
Gave place unto Lovell's fine folly,
    The birds and sweet flowers of May.

Here Venus attends with her lovers,
   Here Floras their suitors betray,
And uncommon secrets discover,
   Which break from the bosom of May.

Here ever young Hebe sits smiling,
   The wonders of youth to portray;
Excluding old age from defeating
   The lads and the lasses of May.

Call in little stranger one minute,
   Your joy will reward your delay;
Come feast with the lark and the linnet,
   And drink of the waters of May.

Walk in little mistress, be steady,
   You're welcome a visit to pay;
All things in the chamber are ready,
   Resolve to be married in May.

GEORGE MOSES HORTON, MYSELF.

I feel myself in need
   Of the inspiring strains of ancient lore,
My heart to lift, my empty mind to feed,
   And all the world explore.

I know that I am old
   And never can recover what is past,
But for the future may some light unfold
   And soar from ages blast.

I feel resolved to try,
   My wish to prove, my calling to pursue,
Or mount up from the earth into the sky,
   To show what Heaven can do.

My genius from a boy,
   Has fluttered like a bird within my heart;
But could not thus confined her powers employ,
   Impatient to depart.

She like a restless bird,
   Would spread her wing, her power to be unfurl'd,
And let her songs be loudly heard,
   And dart from world to world.

A DIRGE.

Hast thou gone and left me
Void of faults but strictly true.
      Fly far away
      Without delay;
Adieu my love, adieu.

Hast thou gone and left me,
Hence to seek another bride;
      I must be still,
      Thou hast thy will;
The world is free and wide.

Only had'st thou told me,
Ere I drunk the bitter cup,
      I could with shame
      Now bear the blame,
And freely give thee up.

But I'm left to ponder,
Now in the depth of sorrow's gloom,
    Like some dull sprite
    In dead of night,
Bewailing o'er her tomb.

Swiftly fly and welcome,
It is the fate of fools to-part,
    With whom I know
    Wedlock is wo,
Without the streams of love.

Where constant love is wanting,
Pleasure has not long to dwell,
    I view my fate,
    Alas, too late,
So Henry fare thee well.

But my love remember,
Hence we meet, and face to face,
    Thy heart shall ache,
    Thy soul shall quake,
Thou wretch of all disgrace.

DEATH OF A FAVORITE.

O death, thy power I own,
  Whose mission was to crush,
And snatch the rose so quickly blown
  Down from its native bush,
The flowers of beauty doomed to pine,
Ascends from this to worlds divine.

Death is a joyful doom;
  Let tears of sorrow dry.
The rose on earth but fades to bloom
  And blossom in the sky;
Why should the soul resist the hand
That leads her to celestial land.

Then bonny bird farewell,
  Till hence we meet again,
Perhaps I have not long to dwell
  Within this cumbrous chain.
Till on Elysian shores we meet,
Till grief is lost and joy complete.

THE FEARFUL TRAVELLER IN THE HAUNTED CASTLE.

Oft do I hear those windows ope
  And shut with dread surprise,
And spirits murmur as they grope,
  But break not on the eyes.

Still fancy spies the winding sheet,
  The phantom and the shroud,
And bids the pulse of horror beat
  Throughout my ears aloud.

Some unknown finger thumps the door,
  From one of falt'ring voice,
Till some one seems to walk the floor
  With an alarming noise.

The drum of horror holds her sound,
    Which will not let me sleep,
When ghastly breezes float around,
    And hidden goblins creep.

Methinks I hear some constant groan,
    The din of all the dead,
While trembling thus I lie alone,
    Upon this restless bed.

At length the blaze of morning broke
    On my impatient view,
And truth or fancy told the joke,
    And bade the night adieu.

'Twas but the noise of prowling rats,
    Which ran with all their speed,
Pursued in haste by hungry cats,
    Which on the vermin feed.

The cat growl'd as she held her prey,
    Which shrieked with all its might,
And drove the balm of sleep away
    Throughout the live-long night.

Those creatures crumbling off the cheese,
    Which on the table lay,
Some cats too quick the rogues to seize,
    With rumbling lost their prey.

Thus man is often, his own self,
    Who makes the night his ghost,
And shrinks with horror from himself,
    Which is to fear the most.

TO CATHERINE.

I'll love thee as long as I live,
   Whate'er thy condition may be
All else but my life would I give
   That thou wast as partial to me.

I love thee because thou art fair,
   And fancy no other beside,
I languish thy pleasures to share,
   Whatever my life may betide.

I'll love thee when youth's vital beam
   Grows dim in the visage of cares,
And trace back in time's rapid stream,
   Thy beauty when sinking in years.

Though nature no longer is gay
   With blooms which the simple adore;
Let virtue forbid me to say
   That Catherine is lovely no more.

THE SWAN—VAIN PLEASURES.

The Swan, which boasted 'mid the tide,
   Whose nest was guarded by the waves,
Floated for pleasure till she died,
   And sunk beneath the flood to lave.

The bird of fashion drops her wing;
   The rose-bush now declines to bloom;
The gentle breezes of the Spring
   No longer waft a sweet perfume.

Fair beauty with those lovely eyes,
    Withers along her vital stream;
Proud fortune leaves her throne and flies
    From pleasure as a flattering dream.

The eagle of exalted fame,
    Which spread her pinions far to sail,
Struggled to fan his dying flame,
    Till pleasure palled in every gale.

And gaudy mammon, sordid gain,
    Whose plume has faded, once so gay,
Languishes 'mid her flowery train,
    While pleasure flies like fumes away.

Vain pleasure, O how short to last,
    Like leaves which quick to ashes burn,
Which kindle from the slightest blast,
    And slight to nothing hence return.

GEN. GRANT—THE HERO OF THE WAR.

Brave Grant, thou hero of the war,
Thou art the emblem of the morning star,
Transpiring from the East to banish fear,
Revolving o'er a servile Hemisphere,
At large thou hast sustained the chief command
And at whose order all must rise and stand,
To hold position in the field is thine,
To sink in darkness or to rise and shine.

Thou art the leader of the Fed'ral band,
To send them at thy pleasure through the land,
Whose martial soldiers never did recoil
Nor fail in any place to take the spoil,
Thus organized was all the army firm,
And led unwavering to their lawful term,
Never repulsed or made to shrink with fear,
Advancing in their cause so truly dear.

The love of Union burned in every heart,
Which led them true and faithful from the start,
Whether upon water or on land,
They all obeyed their marshal's strict command,
By him the regiments were all surveyed,
His trumpet voice was by the whole obeyed,
His order right was every line to form,
And all be well prepared to front the storm.

Ye Southern gentlemen must grant him praise,
Nor on the flag of Union fail to gaze;
Ye ladies of the South forego the prize,
Our chief commander here to recognize,
From him the stream of general orders flow,
And every chief on him some praise bestow,
The well-known victor of the mighty cause
Demands from every voice a loud applause.

What more has great Napoleon ever done,
Though many battles in his course he won?
What more has Alexander e'er achieved,
Who left depopulated cities grieved?
To him we dedicate the whole in song,
The verses from our pen to him belong,
To him the Union banners are unfurled,
The star of peace the standard of the world.

THE POWERS OF LOVE.

It lifts the poor man from his cell
    To fortune's bright alcove,
Its mighty sway few, few can tell,
Mid envious foes it conquers ill,
    There's nothing half like love.

To weary strangers void of rest,
    Who late through life have strove,
Like the bird which seeks its nest,
If you would hence in truth be blest,
    Light on the bough of love

The vagrant plebian void of friends,
    Constrained through wilds to rove,
On this his safety whole depends,
One faithful smile his trouble ends,
    A smile of constant love.

Thus did a captured wretch complain,
    Imploring Heaven above,
Till one with sympathetic pain,
Flew to his arms and broke the chain,
    And grief took flight from love.

Let clouds of danger rise and roar,
    And hope's firm pillars move,
With storms behind and death before,
O, grant me this I crave no more,
    There's nothing half like love.

When nature wakes soft pity's coo,
    The lark deserts the dove,
Compassion melts the creature through,
With palpitation felt by few,
    The wrecking throbs of love.

Let surly discord take its flight
  From wedlock's peaceful grove,
While Union breaks the arm of fight,
With darkness swallowed up in light,
  O, what is there like love.

TO A DEPARTING FAVORITE.

Thou mayst retire but think of me,
  When thou art gone afar,
Where'er in life thy travels be,
If tost along the brackish sea,
  Or borne upon the car.

Thou mayst retire I care not where,
  Thy name my theme shall be,
With thee in heart I shall be there,
Content thy good or ill to share,
  If dared to lodge with thee.

Thou mayst retire beyond thee deep
  And leave thy sister train,
To roam the wilds where dangers sleep,
And leave affection sad to weep
  In bitterness and pain.

Thou mayst retire and yet be glad,
  To leave me thus alone,
Lamenting and bewailing sad :
Farewell, thy sunk deluded lad,
  May rise when thou art gone.

SHERMAN THE GREAT.

He is a victor, and his name
   Shall fly through the world,
From whom the Rebels fly in shame,
Who hence shall bear the torch of fame,
   Till States to naught are hurled.

He has pervaded all the west,
   'Mid thunder, wind and rain ;
Their States could not support the test,
They left their towns at his behest,
   To languish and bewail.

From his approach at once they fled,
   And did not dare to fight,
But left their homes at his behest ;
When once the sad report had spread,
   Their hosts resumed their flight.

Brave Sherman, with thy doubtless host,
   Before whom none can stand,
The rich, the proud forbear to boast,
For the Confedarate powers are lost
   And left without command.

He has led his armies south and east,
   And left his name behind,
Inviting his foes with him to feast
And did not imitate the beast,
   But acted brave and kind.

'Twas not his wish to crush and kill,
   By thus to show his power,
Life to destroy was not his will,
But right and justice to fulfill
   And make his foes to cower.

Brave Sherman, great, exalted man,
  Thou who spread alarm before,
An sent them flying as from pan,
And bade them save your lives who can ;
  Retreat and do no more.

THE HEROES OF THE LATE WAR.

Then fame throughout the land is spread,
  Who o'er the rebels bore the sway ;
The lambs have struck the lions dead
  And taken falseright stores away.

Their names shall live from age to age
  And flourish in unfading prime,
Till nature's beauties shall assuage
  And languish from the death of time.

In thunder let the pean war,
  The trumpet of the northern bands,
And bid the vassal doubt no more,
  That grovelled hopeless thro' the land.

O liberty, forbear to weep,
  Thy hostile cloud will soon be o'er,
For sure thy God forbears to sleep
  Or slumber on the western shore.

We homage pay to friends so dear,
  And lowly cower at their feet ;
We trace them with a smile and tear,
  And sing, the conquest is replete.

Yes, yes, replete with freedom's fire,
   Fought for so faithful night and day,
Who wrung our transports from the lyre;
   Arise my friends and come away.

THE SOUTHERN REFUGEE.

What sudden ill the world await,
   From my dear residence I roam;
I must deplore the bitter fate,
   To straggle from my native home.

The verdant willow droops her head,
   And seems to bid a fare thee well;
The flowers with tears their fragance shed,
   Alas! their parting tale to tell.

'Tis like the loss of Paradise,
   Or Eden's garden left in gloom,
Where grief affords us no device,
   Such is thy lot, my native home.

I never, never shall forget,
   My sad departure far away,
Until the sun of life is set,
   And leaves behind no beam of day.

How can I from my seat remove
   And leave my ever devoted home,
And the dear garden which I love,
   The beauty of my native home.

Alas! sequestered, set aside,
  It is a mournful tale to tell;
'Tis like a lone deserted bride
  That bade her bridegroom fare thee well.

I trust I soon shall dry the tear
  And leave forever hence to roam,
Far from a residence so dear,
  The place of beauty—my native home.

THE SLAVE.

What right divine has mortal man received,
  To domineer with uncontroll'd command?
What philosophic wight has thus believed
  That Heaven entailed on him the weaker band?

If Africa was fraught with weaker light,
  Whilst to the tribes of Europe more was given,
Does this impart to them a lawful right
  To counterfeit the golden rule of Heaven?

Did sovereign justice give to robbery birth,
  And bid the fools to theft their rights betray,
To spread the seeds of slavery o'er the earth,
  That you should hold them as your lawful prey?

Why did the Almighty God the land divide,
  And bid each nation to maintain her own,
Rolling between the deep, the wind and tide,
  With all their rage to make his order known?

The sad phylactory bound on rebel Cain,
  For killing Abel is in blood reveal'd,
For which the soldier falls among the slain,
  A victim on the sanguinary field.

Thus, in the cause of vile and sordid gain ;
  To gratify their lust is all the plea ;
Like Cain you 've your consanguine brother slain,
  And robbed him of his birthright—Liberty.

Why do ye not the Ishmealites enslave,
  Or artful red man in his rude attire,
As well as with the Black man, split the wave,
  And to his progeny with rage aspire.

Because the brood-sow's left side pigs were black,
  Whose sable tincture was by nature struck,
Are you by justice bound to pull them back
  And leave the sandy colored pigs to suck ?

Or can you deem that God does not intend
  His kingdom through creation to display,
The sacred right of nature to defend,
  And show to mortals who shall bear the sway ?

Then suffer Heaven to vindicate the cause ;
  The wrong abolish and the right restore ;
To make a sacrifice of cruel laws,
  And slavish murmurs will be heard no more.

FARE THEE WELL, BUT NOT FOREVER.

Fare thee well, but not forever,
  For we sure shall meet again ;
'Tis not to part and meet more never,
  For pleasure rises out of pain.

I go alas! but know not whither,
   A tear is mixed with every smile,
For sweet and bitter flow together,
   Then let us pause and think awhile.

I leave with thee my heart and treasure,
   Lest thou shouldst thy friend forget,
Thy presence is my only pleasure,
   I was thy friend, and am 'till yet.

Sweet is meeting after parting,
   All's that from bitter flows,
The sting is only fresh when starting,
   It then begins but soon to close.

I never have of peace bereft thee,
   But to cheer thee did I strive;
I was annoyed when first I left thee,
   But trust to meet thee soon alive.

Fare thee well, but not forever,
   Hence we shall together dwell;
Nothing shall our union sever,
   For a moment fare thee well.

THE TRAVELLER.

When from my native clime,
   'Mid lonely valleys pensive far I roam,
'Mid rocks and hills where waters roll sublime,
   'Tis sweet to think of home.

My retrospective gaze
  Bounds on a dark horizon far behind,
But yet the stars of homely pleasure blaze,
  And glimmer on my mind.

When pealing thunders roll,
  And ruffian winds howl threat'ning life with gloom,
To Heaven's kind hand I then commit the whole,
  And smile to think of home.

But cease my pensive soul
  To languish at departure's gloomy shrine,
Still look in front and hail the joyful goal,
  The pleasure teeming line.

When on the deep wide sea
  I wander sailing mid the swelling foam,
Lost from the land by many a long degree,
  O! then I think of home.

I never shall forget,
  The bye-gone pleasures of my native shore,
Until the sun of life forbears to set,
  And pain is known no more.

When nature seems to weep,
  And life hangs trembling o'er the watery tomb,
Hope lifts her peaceful sail to brave the deep,
  And bids me think of home!

My favorite pigeon rest,
  Nor on the plane of sorrow drop thy train,
But on the bough of hope erect thy nest,
  'Till friends shall meet again.

Though in the hermit's cell,
  Where eager friends to cheer me fail to come,
Where zephyrs seem a joyful tale to tell,
  No thought is sweet but home.

RECENT APPEARANCE OF A LADY.

The joy of meeting one so fair
  Inspires the present stream of song,
    A bonny belle,
    That few excel,
And one with whom, I few compare,
  Though out of sight so long.

It is a cause of much delight,
  When lads and lasses meet again,
    But bonny belle,
    Not long to dwell,
For soon upon the wing of flight
  We haste away in pain.

That long hid form I smile to trace—
  A star emerging out of gloom,
    Exalted belle,
    Whose powers excel,
And draw the heart by every grace,
  The queen of every bloom.

Long out of sight, but still in mind,
  Eternal mem'ry holds its grasp,
    Still bonny belle,
    'Tis sweet to tell
Of thee, when I am left behind,
  In sorrow's lonely clasp.

MEDITATIONS ON A COLD DARK AND RAINY NIGHT.

Sweet on the house top falls the gentle shower,
When jet black darkness crowns the silent hour,
When shrill the owlet pours her hollow tone,
Like some lost child sequestered and alone,
When wills bewildering wisp begins to flare,
And Philomela breathes her dulcet air,
'Tis sweet to listen to her nightly tune,
Deprived of starlight on the smiling moon.

When deadly winds sweep round the rural shed,
And tell of strangers lost without a bed,
Fond sympathy invokes her dol'rous lay,
And pleasure steals in sorrow's gloom away,
Till fost'ring Somnus bids my eyes to close,
And smiling visions open to repose;
Still on my soothing couch I lie at ease,
Still round my chamber flows the whistling breeze.

Still in the chain of life I lie confin'd,
To all the threat'ning ills of life resigned;
Regardless of the wandering elfs of night,
While phantoms break on my immortal sight;
The trump of morning bids my slumber end,
While from a flood of light I straight ascend,
When on a busy world I cast my eye,
And think of nightly slumbers with surprise.

GEN'L KILPATRICK, THE BOLD CAVALIER.

Brave wight forever live,
   The pride and glory of thy native State;
Too brave to die, for life must time survive,
   For joys thy end await.
Quick to his post the warrior sped,
Without the slightest shade of dread,
He waves his bright shield o'er the dead;
   Regardless of his life,
At once he spurns the rebels harm
And hurls the thunder with his arm,
   And quells the rage of strife.

At once he shocks his foe
   And drives the rebel troops without delay,
While scattering numbers fall beneath the blow,
   And horsemen fleet away.
He strikes the cities of renown,
And throws the walls and cities down;
He speeds his way thro' ev'ry town,
   In storm by night and day,.
The blaze of wrath he kindles higher,
And mounds dissolve beneath the fire,
   Their folly to betray.

Eternal brave remain
   And live immortal to the end of time,
And boast without occasion to complain,
   But still ascend sublime.
Ye bards of victory, lift the pen
And shout and hail the chief of men,
He rises not to fall again,

As in unfading prime;
Away let slavery fly us smoke,
The cloud which must the heavens provoke,
　To curse the survile clime.

What shall this man deplume,
　Who towers above and leaves the clouds below:
Bold cavalier, thro' time forever bloom,
　Thy skill in war to show.
Let freedom's sons the trumpet sound
Aloud, and spread the triumph round,
And sing, rise brothers from the ground,
　And brave the inveterate foe;
His nimble brute is like a star,
The martial steed, the horse of war
　Defies the lurking foe.

LINCOLN IS DEAD.

He is gone, the strong base of the nation,
　The dove to his covet has fled;
Ye heroes lament his privation,
　For Lincoln is dead.

He is gone down, the sun of the Union,
　Like Pheobus, that sets in the west;
The planet of peace and commotion,
　Forever has gone to his rest.

He is gone from a world of commotion,
　No equal succeeds in his stead;
His wonders extend with the ocean,
　Whose waves murmur, Lincoln is dead.

He is gone and can ne'er be forgotten,
   Whose great deeds eternal shall bloom;
When gold, pearls and diamonds are rotten,
   His deeds will break fresh from the tomb.

He is gone out of glory to glory,
   A smile with the tear may be shed;
O, then let us tell the sweet story,
   Triumphantly, Lincoln is dead.

ON AN OLD DELUDED SUITOR.

See sad deluded love in years too late,
With tears desponding o'er the tomb of fate;
While dusky evening's veil excludes the light,
Which in the morning broke upon his sight.
He now regrets his vain, his fruitless plan,
And sadly wonders at the faults of man;
'Tis now from beauty's torch he wheels aside,
And strives to soar above affection's tide;
'Tis now that sorrow feeds the worm of pain,
With tears which never can the loss regain;
'Tis now he drinks the wormwood and the gall,
And all the sweets of early pleasure pall;
When from his breast the hope of fortune flies,
The songs of transport languish into sighs.
Fond lovely rose that beamed as she blew,
Of all the charms of youth the most untrue;
She with delusive smiles prevail'd to move,
This silly heart into the snares of love.
Then like a flower closed against the bee,
Folds her arms and turns her back on me;

When in my fancy's lyre her smile she shed,
The torch by which deluded love was led.
Then like a lark from boyhood's maze I soared,
And thus in song her flattering smiles adored;
My heart was then by fondling love betray'd,
A thousand pleasures bloomed but soon to fade;
From joy to joy my heart exulting flew,
In quest of one though fair, yet far from true.

THE WOODMAN AND THE MONEY HUNTER.

Throughout our rambles much we find,
   The bee tree bursts with honey;
Wild birds we tame of ev'ry kind,
At once they seem to be resigned;
I know but one that lags behind—
   There's nothing lags but money.

The wood affords us much supply,
   The opossum, coon and coney;
They are all tame and venture nigh,
Regardless of the public eye;
I know but one among them shy,
   There's nothing shy but money.

And she lies in the bankrupt shade,
   The cunning fox is funny;
When thus the public debts are paid,
Deceitful cash is not afraid,
Where funds are hid for private trade,
   There's nothing paid but money.

Then let us roam the woods along,
  And drive the coon and coney;
Our lead is good, our powder strong,
To shoot the pigeons as they throng,
But sing no more the idle song,
  Nor prowl the chase for money.

THE EYE OF LOVE.

I know her story-telling eye
  Has more expression than her tongue,
And from that heart extorted sigh,
  At once the peal of love is rung.

When that soft eye lets fall a tear
  Of doating fondness as we part,
The stream is from a cause sincere,
  And gushes from a melting heart.

What! shall her flutt'ring pulse restrain
  The life-watch beating from her soul,
When all the power of hate is slain,
  And love permits it no control?

When said, her tongue, I wish thee well,
  Her eye declares it must be true,
And every sentence seemed to tell
  The tale of sorrow told by few.

When low she bow'd and wheel'd aside,
  I saw her blushing temples fade;
Her smiles were sunk in sorrow's tide,
  But love was in her eye betray'd.

THE CREDITOR TO HIS PROUD DEBTOR.

Ha! tott'ring Johnny strut and boast,
But think of what your feathers cost;
Your crowing days are short at most,
   You bloom but soon to fade.
Surely you could not stand so wide,
If strictly to the bottom tried;
The wind would blow your plume aside,
   If half your debts were paid.
     Then boast and bear the crack,
     With the Sheriff at your back,
     Huzza for dandy Jack,
     My jolly fop, my Jo—

The blue smoke from your segar flies,
Offensive to my nose and eyes,
The most of people would be wise,
   Your presence to evade.
Your pockets jingle loud with cash,
And thus you cut a foppish dash,
But alas! dear boy, you would be trash,
   If your accounts were paid.
     Then boast and bear the crack, &c.

My duck bill boots would look as bright,
Had you in justice served me right,
Like you, I then could step as light,
   Before a flaunting maid.
As nicely could I clear my throat,
And to my tights, my eyes devote,
But I'd leave you bear, without coat,
   For which you have not paid.
     Then boast and bear the crack, &c.

I'd toss myself with a scornful air,
And to a poor man pay no care,
I could rock cross-legged in my chair,
   Within the cloister shade.
I'd gird my neck with a light cravat,
And creaming wear my bell-crown hat ;
But away my down would fly at that,
   If once my debts were paid.
      Then boast and bear the crack,
      With the Sheriff at your back,
      Huzza for dandy Jack,
      My jolly fop, my Jo—

PLEASURES OF HOPE.

As smoke from a volcano soars in the air,
   The soul of man discontent mounts from a sigh,
Exhaled as to Heaven in mystical prayer,
   Invoking that love which forbids him to die.

Sweet hope, lovely passion my grief ever chase,
   And scatter the gloom which veils pleasures bright ray,
O ! lend me thy wings and assist me to trace
   The flight of my own fair one when gone far away.

When the dim star of pleasure sets glimmering alone,
   The planet of beauty on life's dreary shore,
And the fair bird of fancy forever is flown,
   On pinions of haste to be heard of no more.

Hope, tell me, dear passion, thou wilt not forget,
   To flourish still sweetly and blossom as gay,
Expelling like morning the gloom of regret,
   When the lark of affection is gone far away.

If hurried into some unchangeable clime,
   Where oceans of pleasure continually roll,
Far, far, from the limited borders of time,
   With a total division of body and soul.

Hope, tell me, dear passion, which must earth survive,
   That love will be sweeter when nature is o'er,
And still without pain through eternity live,
   In the triumph of pleasure when time is no more?

O! love when the daylight of pleasure shall close,
   Let the vesper of death break on life's dusky even,
Let the faint sun of time set in peace as it rose,
   And eternity open thy morning in Heaven.

Then hope, lovely passion, thy torch shall expire,
   Effusing on nature life's last feeble ray,
While the night-maid of love sets her taper on fire,
   To guard smiling beauty from time far away.

A SLAVE'S REFLECTIONS THE EVE BEFORE HIS SALE.

O, comrades! to-morrow we try,
   The fate of an exit unknowing—
Tears trickled from every eye—
   'Tis going, 'tis going, 'tis going!

Who shall the dark problem then solve,
   An evening of gladness or sorrow,
Thick clouds of emotion evolve,
   The sun which awaits us to-morrow,
   O! to-morrow! to-morrow!
Thick clouds of emotion evolve,
   The sun which awaits us to-morrow.

Soon either with smiles or with tears,
  Will the end of our course be completed,
The progress of long fleeting years,
  Triumphant or sadly regretted.

In whom shall the vassal confide,
  On a passage so treacherous and narrow,
What tongue shall the question decide,
  The end which awaits us to-morrow?
  O! to-morrow, to-morrow!
What tongue shall the question decide,
  The end which awaits us to-morrow?

The sun seems with doubt to look down,
  As he rides on his chariot of glory,
A king with a torch and a crown,
  But fears to exhibit his story.

What pen the condition makes known,
  O! prophet thy light would I borrow,
To steer through the desert alone,
  And gaze on the fate of to-morrow;
  O! to-morrow, to-morrow!
To steer through the desert alone,
  And gaze on the fate of to-morrow.

FAREWELL TO FRANCES.

Farewell! If ne'er I see thee more,
  Though distant calls my flight impel,
I shall not less thy grace adore,
  So friend forever fare thee well.

Farewell forever did I say?
  What! never more thy face to see?
Then take the last fond look to-day,
  And still to-morrow think of me.

Farewell, alas! the tragic sound,
  Has many a tender bosom torn,
While desolation spread around,
  Deserted friendship left to mourn.

Farewell, awakes the sleeping tear,
  The dormant rill from sorrow's eye,
Expressed from one by nature dear,
  Whose bosom heaves the latent sigh.

Farewell is but departure's tale,
  When fond association ends,
And fate expands her lofty sail,
  To show the distant flight of friends.

Alas! and if we sure must part,
  Far separated long to dwell,
I leave thee with a broken heart,
  So friend forever fare thee well.

I leave thee, but forget thee never,
  Words cannot my feeling tell,
Fare thee well, and if forever,
  Still forever fare thee well.

THE RETREAT FROM MOSCOW.

Sad Moscow, thy fate do I see,
  Fire, fire, in the city all cry;
Like quails from the eagle all flee,
  Escape in a moment or die.

It looks like the battle of Troy,
  The storm rises higher and higher;
The scene of destruction all hearts must annoy,
  The whirlwinds, the smoke and the fire.

The dread conflagration rolls forth,
  Augmenting the rage of the wind,
Which blows it from south unto north,
  And leaves but the embers behind.

It looks like gomorrah the flame,
  Is moving still nigher and nigher;
Aloud from all quarters the people proclaim,
  The whirlwind, the smoke and the fire.

A dead fumigation now swells,
  A blue circle darkens the air,
With tones as the pealing of bells,
  Farewell to the brave and the fair.

O, Moscow, thou city of grace,
  Consigned to a dread burning pyre,
With morning to ev'ning, with sorrow I trace,
  The whirlwinds, the smoke and the fire.

The dogs in the kennel all howl,
  The wether takes flight with the ox;
Appall'd on the wing is the fowl,
  The pigeon deserting her box.

With a heart full of pain in the night,
  'Mid hillocks and bogs I retire;
Thro' lone deadly vallies I steer by its light,
  The wild storm, the smoke and the fire.

Though far the crash breaks on my ear,
   The stars glimmer dull in the sky;
The shrieks of the women I hear,
   The fall of the kingdom is nigh.

O, Heaven, when earth is no more,
   And all things in nature expire;
May I thus, with safety keep distant before,
   The whirlwind, the smoke and the fire.

IMPLORING TO BE RESIGNED AT DEATH.

Let me die and not tremble at death,
   But smile at the close of my day,
And then at the flight of my breath,
   Like a bird of the morning in may,
        Go chanting away.

Let me die without fear of the dead,
   No horrors my soul shall dismay,
And with faith's pillow under my head,
   With defiance to mortal decay,
        Go chanting away.

Let me die like a son of the brave,
   And martial distinction display;
Nor shrink from a thought of the grave,
   No, but with a smile from the clay,
        Go chanting away.

Let me die glad, regardless of pain,
   No pang to this world betray,
And the spirit cut loose from its chains,
   So loath in the flesh to delay,
        Go chanting away.

Let me die, and my worst foe forgive,
   When death veils the last vital ray;
Since I have but a moment to live,
   Let me, when the last debt I pay,
        Go chanting away.

THE GRADUATE LEAVING COLLEGE.

What summons do I hear,
   The morning peal, departure's knell.
My eyes let fall a friendly tear,
   And bid this place farewell.

Attending servants come,
   The carriage wheels like thunder roar,
To bear the pensive seniors home,
   Here to be seen no more.

Pass one more transient night,
   The morning sweeps the College clean;
The graduate takes his last long flight,
   No more in College seen.

The bee, which courts the flower,
   Must with some pain itself employ,
And then fly, at the day's last hour,
   Home to its hive with joy.

TO THE KING OF MACEDONIA.

PHILIP THOU ART MORTAL.

Thou mayst with pleasure hail the dawn,
   And greet the morning's eye;
Remember King, the night comes on,
The fleeting day will soon be gone,
Nor distant land proclaims the fun'ral tone;
   Philip thou hast to die.

With thee, thy dame the queen of birds,
   May spread her wings to fly,
Or smile to trace the num'rous hords,
Thunders from the Lord of lords;
I hear some peal surpassing human words,
   Philip thou hast to die.

Thou mayst thy mighty host survey,
   And neighboring kings defy,
Whilst round thy retinues flit gay,
Beneath thy pomps imperial ray,
Make merry on the tide of joy to-day,
   To-morrow thou shalt die.

I heave to hear the days last peal,
   A sorrow's teeming sigh;
The mornings fluttering bird has flown,
The roses fade so quickly blown,
The lofty king falls lifeless from his throne,
   Philip was born to die.

'Twas thus the haughty King of France,
   Strove to ascend the sky;
Lifting his adamantine lance,
He bade his dauntless war horse prance,
Defied the world and rode the car of chance,
   To rage, to fume and die.

Thus vile, thus obstinately vain,
   He pours his distant brag;
Regardless of his millions slain,
Regardless his pale surviving train,
Was but wrapped in his infernal chain,
   Dies on the ocean crag.

This faithful lesson read to all
   Creation far and wide;
It is the fate from Adam's fall,
The Swain, the King, the low and tall,
The watchman of the grave must give the call,
   Mortal, thou hast to die.

DIVISION OF AN ESTATE.

It well bespeaks a man beheaded, quite
Divested of the laurel robe of life,
When ev'ry member struggles for its base;
The head, the power of order, now recedes,
Unheeded efforts rise on ev'ry side,
With dull emotion rolling thro' the brain
Of apprehending slaves. The flocks and herds
In sad confusion now run to and fro,
And seem to ask, distressed, the reason why
That they are thus prostrated. Howl, ye dogs!
Ye cattle low! Ye sheep astonish'd bleat!
Ye bristling swine trudge squealing thro' the glades
Void of an owner to impart you food.
Sad horses lift your head and neigh aloud,
And caper, frantic, from the dismal scene;
Mow the last food upon your grass clad lea,
And leave a solitary home behind.

In hopeless widowhood, no longer gay,
The traveling sun of gain his journey ends;
In unavailing pain he sets with tears—
A King, sequestered, sinking from his throne;
Succeeded by a train of busy friends,
Like stars which rise with smiles to mark the flight
Of awful Phœbus to another world.
Stars after stars in fleet succession rise;
Into the wide empire of fortune cleave,
Regardless of the donor of their lamps,
Like heirs forgetful of parental care,
Redound in reverence to expiring age.
But soon parental benediction flies
Like vivid meteors in a moment gone,
As though they ne'er had been; but O, the state,
The dark suspense in which poor vassals stand,
Each mind upon the spire of chance hangs, fluctuate,
The day of separation is at hand.
Imagination lifts her gloomy curtain
Like evening's mantle at the flight of day,
Through which the trembling pinnacle we spy,
On which we soon must stand with hopeful smiles,
Or apprehending frowns to tumble on
The right or left forever.

PRIDE IN HEAVEN.

On Heaven's ethereal plain,
   With hostile rage ambition first begun,
When the arch rebel strove himself to reign,
   And take Jehovah's throne,
Swift to the fight the seraphim,
On floods of pride were seen to swim,
And bold defy the Power Supreme,
   And thus their God disown.

High on a dome of state,
  From azure fields he cast his glaring eye,
Licentious trains his magazines await,
  At whose command they fly;
The gloom excludes celestial charms,
When all the angels rush to arms,
Heaven shakes beneath the vast alarms,
  And earth begins to sigh.

Eternal mountains move,
  And seven fold thunder rock the hills,
While starry throngs desert the worlds above, oelow,
  Beneath Jehovah's brow.
O Lucifer! thou mourning son,
To glut thy pride what hast thou done?
Sing O, ye Heavens, the plague is gone,
  And weep thou earth for woe.

Creation felt the fall,
  And trembling nature heav'd a dismal groan,
For that rebellion brought her into thrall,
  She must her fate bemoan;
See angels fall no more to rise,
And feed the worm that never dies,
No ear of grace can hear their cries,
  And hoarse lamenting tone.

Weak nature lay exposed,
  And felt the wound in pleasing heat concealed,
And void of fear the secret charm dissolved,
  Which every ill revealed;
The venom struck through every vein,
And every creature felt the pain,
But undefiled a lamb was slain,
  By which the wound was healed.

TO MISS TEMPE.

Blessed hope when Tempe takes her last long flight,
   And leaves her last lorn lover to complain,
Like Luna mantling o'er the brow of night,
   Thy glowing wing dispels the gloom of pain.

'Tis wondrous hope when Tempe sails afar,
   Thy vital lamp remains to burn behind,
While by-gone pleasures like a setting star,
   Reflects her glory o'er the twilight mind.

Thy glowing wing was never spread to tire,
   Expanded o'er the mansion of the brave,
To fan and set the heaving breast on fire,
   That soars in triumph from affliction's wave.

Then Tempe dart along the ocean drear,
   Hope yet forbids my cheerful soul to weep,
But marks thy passage with affection's tears,
   And hails thee on the bosom of the deep.

Farewell, since thou wilt leave thy native shore,
   I smile to think that I am not left alone,
Auspicious hope shall yet my peace restore,
   When thou art from the beach forever gone.

MAN, A TORCH.

Blown up with painful care and hard to light,
A glimmering torch blown in a moment out,
Suspended by a web, an angel's bait,
Floating at stake along the stream of chance,

Snatched from its hook by the fish of poverty,
A silent cavern is his last abode,
The king's repository veiled with gloom;
The umbrage of a thousand oziers bowed,
The couch of hallowed bones, the slave's asylum,
The brave's retreat and end of ev'ry grace.

LIKE BROTHERS WE MEET.

DEDICATED TO THE FEDERAL AND LATE CONFEDERATE SOLDIERS.

Like heart-loving brothers we meet,
   And still the loud thunders of strife,
The blaze of fraternity kindles most sweet,
   There's nothing more pleasing in life.

The black cloud of faction retreats,
   The poor is no longer depressed,
See those once discarded resuming their seats,
   The lost strangers soon will find rest.

The soldier no longer shall roam,
   But soon shall land safely ashore,
Each soon will arrive at his own native home,
   And struggle in warfare no more.

The union of brothers is sweet,
   Whose wives and children do come,
Their sons and fair daughters with pleasure they greet,
   When long absent fathers come home.

They never shall languish again,
   Nor discord their union shall break,
When brothers no longer lament and complain,
   Hence never each other forsake.

Hang closely together like friends,
  By peace killing foes never driven,
The storm of commotion eternally ends,
  And earth will soon turn into Heaven.

THE DYING SOLDIER'S MESSAGE.

Weep mother, weep, it must be so,
  A tear when parting must be shed,
  The falling tribute is due the dead,
Which leaves the world in gloom below.
  Go flitting bird that splits the sky,
Where sits my mother sighing,
  And should she rise and ask you why,
O, tell her I am dying.

Weep, Father, I shall soon be gone;
  I travel to return no more,
  But sorrow cannot life restore,
I leave the whole to God alone.
  Go, gentle zephyrs, bear the tale,
While sweet the dove is sighing,
  Tell mother never long bewail,
However, I am dying.

Weep, brother, for fraternal love,
  Death is about to close the scene—
  Short is the space that lies between
My soul and better worlds above.
  Let thunder storms my fate betray,
Ye sable vapors flying,
  Sound that my life has past away,
Tell mother I am dying.

Weep, sister, love was born to grieve
  For one thus passing out of time;
  From this to other worlds sublime,
I shut my eyes and take my leave.
  The favorite bird will soon have fled;
The fate there's no denying,
  I soon shall lodge among the dead,
For I am surely dying.

THE TREACHEROUS WOMAN.

Woman, thou bloom of every danger,
  From whose charms my sorrows rise,
To thee I'd live and die a stranger;
  He who shuns thee must be wise.

Thy dearest friend is just to doubt thee,
  Wise to shun thy hidden snare;
Man is better far without thee,
  So deceitful, tho' so fair.

To sport with thee, it is but folly,
  Causing many a bitter sigh;
Why, fondness leads to melancholy
  And leaves a hopeful wretch to die.

Then, let every wise endeavor
  Be thy fondness to evade,
From one slight touch I'm gone forever;
  With once my trust in thee betray'd.

THE SPECTATOR OF THE BATTLE OF BELMONT, NOVEMBER 6, 1863.

O, brother spectators, I long shall remember,
   The blood-crimson veil which spreads over the field,
When battle commenc'd on the sixth of November,
   With war-beaming aspect, the sword and the shield.

The sound of destruction breaks loud from the mortars,
   The watchman is tolling the death-tuning knell,
The heroes are clustering from quarter to quarter;
   What mortal, the fate of this combat shall tell?

Blood breaks from its vein like a stream from its fountain;
   Spectators the pain of the conflict explore;
The fugitives fly to the cave on the mountain,
   Betray'd by the vestige of blood in their gore.

The conflict begins from the twang of the drummer,
   And ends with the peal of a tragical tale;
O yes, it subsides like a storm into summer,
   No less for the dead shall the living bewail.

I've heard of the battles of many foreign nations;
   I've heard of the wonderful conflict of Troy,
And battles, with bloodshed, thro' all generations,
   But nothing like this could my feelings annoy.

The dark dirge of destiny, sung by a spirit,
   Alone can the scene of the combat display,
For surely no dull earthly mortal can merit
   A wonder to equal this tragical lay.

LIBERTY.

O, Liberty, thou dove of peace,
   We must aspire to thee,
Whose wings thy pinions must release,
   And fan Columbia free.

The torpid reptile in the dust,
   Moves active from thy glee,
And own the declamation just,
   That nations should be free.

Ye distant isles espouse the theme,
   Far, far, beyond the sea ;
The sun declares in every beam,
   All nations should be free.

Hence, let Brittania rage no more,
   Distressing vapors flee,
And bear the news from shore to shore,
   Columbia, still be free.

EXECUTION OF PRIVATE HENRY ANDERSON,
Co. D., 9th Mich. Cav. Vols., at Lexington, North Carolina, May 13th, 1865.

This verse is plain, that all may understand,
The scene is solemn and expressly grand ;
The must'ring concourse form'd in grand array,
Betrayed the fate of the expiring day ;
Gazing spectators seemed completely dumb,
Beneath the sound of bugle and the drum.

The fun'ral march attracted every eye,
To see the trembling malefactor die;
O, memorable eve, not soon forgot,
'Tis written on a tablet ne'er to blot;
We never can the scene portray,
The ghastly aspect of the fatal day.

We've heard of martyrs at the cruel stake,
From which an adamantine heart would break;
We've heard of victims on the fun'ral pyre,
Containing sacrifice and set on fire,
When victims died beneath the ruthless flame,
The brutal torture of eternal shame.

This seems to bear the mark, tho' justly done,
A case that every sober man may shun;
'Twas for the deed of open homicide,
This guilty malefactor fell and died.
See well arrayed the attentive squadrons stand,
Thus to discharge their guns at one command;
'Till pointing at one mark the shaft of death,
He breathes at once his last decisive breath.

It is, indeed, a sad infernal crime
To one's own self, thus hurried out of time;
He introduces first the murderous strife,
By his own hand he spurns away his life!
How many creatures thus have fell,
Imbibing nectar from the bowls of hell!

Inspiring depredations all the night,
And thus betrayed the death at morning light;
Thus flies the deadly shaft without control—
He fell upon his coffin, O, my soul!
Let all that live the scene appall—
He dies! no more to live at all, at all!

A DIRGE ON THE SAME.

Look! my soul, O, look and wonder!
  Tears distil from every eye;
Soul and body torn asunder—
  What a dreadful death I die!

Hark! the knell of death is tolling!
  Just before me lies the grave!
For the pain there's no controlling—
  Shoot! I fall! no longer brave!

By a martial host surrounded,
  What a dreadful sight to see!
All my hopes are now confounded,
  Say, what will become of me?

Hark! I hear the death drum beating!
  Every pleasure sinks in gloom;
Doleful music still repeating—
  Drag the culprit in his tomb!

Void of father or a mother
  In this land, to take my part;
Void of sister or a brother
  To appease my broken heart.

Hark! I hear imperial rebels
  Rattling in accursed chains;
Crowded by a group of devils
  Wailing in eternal pain!

THE GUILTY JUDGE.

That thoughtless soul 'tis hard to find,
　Not guilty of some dirty plan,
Utters the charge, yet breaks behind—
　　Thou art the man!

Then hush'd the Judge's trump so shrill,
　Let every mortal live that can;
Detecting fraud, I hear it thrill—
　　Thou art the man!

Such guilty wights were ever found
　Since the creation first began;
We hear the trump of conscience sound—
　　Thou art the man!

Take care, my soul, what lacks within,
　Nor cast my friend in battle's van;
And hear, whilst I upbraid the same—
　　Thou art the man!

Some coward may lend the deed a wing
　The cruel blaze of guilt to fan;
To them the sounding wheel distinct—
　　Thou art the man!

By whom the Saviour was betrayed
　To death, from which he rose again,
And tells thee while power arrayed—
　　Thou art the man!

How oft I frown upon the same,
　Or whether in some gloomy plan,
'Tis written on my heart the same—
　　Thou art the man!

The man, while on life's flatt'ring wave,
  Who next shall close another span;
Some voice may answer from the grave—
  Thou art the man!

THE FLAG OF THE FREE.

It is enough, the flag lift high,
  Effuse the stream of jubilee;
Proclaim aloud in earth and sky,
  The flag floats over the free.

It is enough, who would be sad,
  Let it be spread by land and sea,
The Union is in honor clad,
  The flag floats over the free.

The flag is spread, the storm is o'er,
  The echo's break the vast decree;
The soldiers cease and fight no more,
  The flag floats over the free.

Lift up thy head, exhausted slave,
  Nor to the woods for shelter flee;
Vain shall the threat'ning tyrant save,
  The flag floats over the free.

Come home then straggling wretch, come home,
  And from a rebel scorn to flee;
No more thro' sultry valley's roam,
  The flag floats over the free.

No longer let the sighs be heard,
   From vassals on the bended knee;
Forbidden to return a word,
   The flag floats over the free.

ONE GENERATION PASSETH AWAY AND ANOTHER COMETH.

From world to world, unknown we speed,
   And leave the globe where first we try;
While others to our place succeed,
   And in a moment die.

Alas, we know not whence we came,
   To tarry but a transient day;
Break into time to gather fame,
   And pass at once away.

At once we rise and fix our snares,
   To catch the flitting birds of gain;
'Till burdened with a thousand cares,
   And life turns into pain.

Vain bird, a while think what am I,
   Here entering 'mid a hawk-like throng;
Quickly hatched out, as quick to fly,
   And dare not tarry long.

Where is the mighty and the stout,
   Who lived this fading world to crave;
Left and forever gone without,
   A stone to show their grave.*

---

* Psalm 37, v. 36.

A VISIT TO MY MOTHER'S GRAVE.

When zephyrs poured the doleful sound,
    Like spirits from some fun'ral cave,
I 'mid the dormitory found,
    My mother's lonely grave.

I must the hallowed spot endear,
    Beneath the swell of sorrow's grave,
The scene awakes a filial tear,
    My mother's lonely grave.

Let me her dust with smiles resign,
    Nor let my locks in sorrow lave,
While bending o'er the sacred sign,
    My mother's lonely grave.

My eyes were still in sorrow drowned,
    Which bends the stout and stills the brave,
And I in silence left behind,
    My mother's lonely grave.

Farewell, my dearest friend awhile,
    I have no good on earth to crave;
On thee, O let me drop a smile,
    My mother's lonely grave.

DEATH OF AN OLD CARRIAGE HORSE.

I was a harness horse,
    Constrained to travel weak or strong,
With orders from oppressing force,
    Push along, push along.

I had no space of rest,
   And took at forks the roughest prong,
Still by the cruel driver pressed,
   Push along, push along.

Vain strove the idle bird,
   To charm me with her artless song,
But pleasure lingered from the word,
   Push along, push along.

The order of the day
   Was push, the peal of every tongue,
The only word was all the way,
   Push along, push along.

Thus to my journey's end,
   Had I to travel right or wrong,
'Till death my sweet and favored friend,
   Bade me from life to push along.

THE RISING SUN.

The king of day rides on,
   To give the placid morning light;
On wheels of glory moves his throne,
   Whose light adorns the earth.

When once his limpid maid
   Has the imperial course begun,
The lark deserts the dusky shade,
   And soars to meet the sun.

Up from the orient deep
   Aurora comes without delay,
With brooms of light the shade to sweep,
   And drive the gloom away.

Ye ghostly scenes give way,
   Our king is coming now in sight,
Beaming the diadem of day,
   Whose crest expels the night.

Thus we, like birds, retreat
   To groves, and hide from every eye;
Our slumbering dust will rise and meet
   Its morning in the sky.

The immaterial sun,
   Now hid within empyreal gloom,
Will break forth in a brighter theme,
   And call us from the tomb.

THE SETTING SUN.

'Tis sweet to trace the setting sun,
   While blushing down the west,
When his diurnal race is run,
The traveler stops the gloom to shun,
   And lodge his bones to rest.

Far from the eye he sinks apace,
   But still throws back his light,
From oceans of resplendent grace,
Whence sleeping vesper paints her face,
   And bids the sun good night.

To those hesperian fields by night
　My thoughts in vision stray,
Like spirits stealing into light,
From gloom upon the wing of flight,
　Soaring from time away.

The eagle with his pinions furl'd
　Takes his departing peep,
And hails the accidental world,
Swift round whose base the globes are whirl'd.
　Whilst weary creatures sleep.

MEMORY.

Sweet memory, like a pleasing dream,
　Still lends a dull and feeble ray;
For ages with her vestige teems,
　When beauty's trace is worn away.

When pleasure, with her harps unstrung,
　Sits silent to be heard no more,
Or leaves them on the willows hung,
　And pastime glee forever o'er.

Still back in smiles thy glory steals,
　With evening dew drops from thine eye;
The twilight bursting from thy wheels,
　Ascends, and bids oblivion fly.

Memory, thy blush prevails to bloom,
　Designed to fade, no, never, never;
We'll stamp thy memory on the tomb.
　And bid th' immortal live forever!

When youth's bright sun has once declined,
　And bid his smiling day expire,
Memory, thy torch steals up behind,
　And sets thy hidden stars on fire.

PROSPERITY.

Come, thou queen of every creature,
　Nature calls thee to her arms,
Love sits gay on every feature,
　Teeming with a thousand charms.

Meet me 'mid the wreathing bowers,
　Greet me in the citron grove,
Where I saw the belle of flowers
　Dealing with the bloom of love.

Hark! the lowly dove of Sharon
　Bids thee rise and come away,
From a vale both dry and barren,
　Come to one where life is gay.

Come, thou queen of all the forest—
　Fair Feronia—mountain glee—
Lovelier than the garden flourish,
　Or the goddess of the bee.

Come, Stercules, and with pleasure
　Fertilize the teeming field,
From thy stran dissolved at leisure,
　Bid the bee her bounty yield.

Come, thou queen of every creature,
  Nature calls thee to her arms,
Love sits gay on every feature,
  Teeming with a thousand charms.

DEATH OF GEN. JACKSON—AN EULOGY.

Hark! from the mighty hero's tomb
  I hear a voice proclaim,
A sound which fills the world with gloom,
  But magnifies his name.

His flight from time let braves deplore,
  And wail from State to State,
And sound abroad from shore to shore,
  The death of one so great.

He scorned to live a captured slave,
  And fought his passage through;
He dies, the prince of all the brave,
  And bids the world adieu.

Sing to the memory of his power,
  Ye vagrant mountaineers;
Ye rustic peasants drop a shower
  Of love for him in tears.

He wields the glittering sword no more,
  With that trans-piercing eye;
Ceases to roam the mountain o'er
  And gets him down to die.

Still let the nation spread his fame,
   While marching from his tomb,
Aloud let all the world proclaim,
   Jackson forever bloom.

No longer to the world confined,
   He goes down like a star,
He sets and leaves his friends behind,
   To rein the steed of war.

Hark! from the mighty hero's tomb
   I hear a voice proclaim,
A sound which fills the world with gloom,
   But magnifies his name.

MR. CLAY'S RECEPTION AT RALEIGH, APRIL, 1844.

Salute the august train, a scene so grand,
   With every tuneful band,
      The mighty brave,
      His country bound to save,
   Extends his aiding hand,
For joy his vot'ries whoop and stamp,
Excited by the blaze of pomp,
      Let every eye
      The scene descry,
   The sons of freedom's land.

They look ten thousand, stars turn their gaze,
   To give the hero praise—
      Immortal Clay,
      The cause is to portray,

Your tuneful voices raise;
The light of Columbian sun,
Breaks from his patriot throne,
    Let all admire,
    The faithful sire,
The chief musician plays.

Ye bustling crowds give way, proclaims the dru
    And give the patriot room,
    The cannon's sound,
    The blast of trumpets bound,
    Be this our father's home,
Now let the best musician play,
A skillful tune for Henry Clay,
    Let every ear,
    With transport hear,
The President is come.

Let sister States greet the Columbian feast,
    With each admiring guest,
    Thou art our choice,
    Let ev'ry joyful voice,
    Sound from the East to West,
Let haughty Albions lion roar,
The eagle must prevail to soar,
    And in lov'ly form,
    Above the storm,
Erect her peaceful nest.

Beyond each empire she throws her eye,
    Which lifted to the sky,
    No thunders roll,
    To agitate her soul,
    Beneath her feet they fly,

Let skillful fingers sweep the lyre,
Strike every ear, set hearts on fire,
  Let monarchs sleep,
  Beyond the deep,
 And howling faction die.

Nor hence forget the scene applauding day,
 When every heart was gay,
  The universal swell,
  Rushed from the loud town bell,
 In awful, grand array,
We see them from the bright parade,
And hark! a gladdening march is played,
  Along the street,
  The theme is sweet,
 For every voice is, Clay.

To the Capitol the low and upland peers,
 Resort with princely fears,
  And homage pay;
  A long huzza for Clay,
 Falls on our ears,
Loud from his lips the thunders roll,
And fill with wonder every soul:
  Round the sire of the State,
  All concentrate,
 And every mortal hears.

CLAY'S DEFEAT.

'Tis the hope of the noble defeated,
 The aim of the marksman is vain,
The wish of destruction completed,
 The soldier eternally slain.

When winter succeeds to the summer,
   The bird is too chilly to sing,
No music is played for the drummer,
   No cawl is heard on the wing.

The court of a nation forsaken,
   An edifice stripped of its dome,
Its fame from her pinnacle shaken,
   Like the sigh heaving downfall of Rome,

Fall'n, fall'n, is the chief of the witty,
   The prince of republican power,
The star-crown of Washington city,
   Descends his political tower.

The gold plated seat is bespoken,
   The brave of the West is before
The bowl at the fountain is broken,
   The music of fame is no more.

No longer a wonderful story
   Is told for the brave whig to hear,
Whose sun leaves his circuit of glory,
   Or sinks from the light of his sphere.

SLAVERY.

Slavery, thou peace-disturbing thief,
   We can't but look with frowns on thee,
Without the balm which gives relief,
   The balm of birthright—Liberty.

Thy wing has been for ages furl'd,
   Thy vessel toss'd from wave to wave,
By stormy winds 'mid billows hurl'd—
   Such is the fate of every slave.

A loathesome burden we are to bear,
   Through sultry bogs we trudging go;
Thy rusty chains we frown to wear,
   Without one inch of wealth to show.

Our fathers from their native land
   Were dragged across the brackish deep,
Bound fast together, hand in hand,
   O! did the God of nature sleep?

When sadly thro' the almond grove
   The pirate dragged them o'er the sod,
Devoid of pity and of love,
   They seemed as left without a God.

Are we not men as well as they,
   Born to enjoy the good of earth,
Brought in creation from the clay,
   To reap a blessing from our birth?

Alas! how can such rebels thrive,
   Who take our lives and wealth away,
Since all were placed on earth to live,
   And prosper by the light of day.

The maledictions of our God,
   Pervade the dwindling world we see;
He hurls the vengeance with his rod,
   And thunders, let the slave be free!

THE TERRORS OF WAR.

He bids the comet play,
   And empires tremble at his burning tail;
Commanding troops without delay,
The distant land his calls obey,
Ye proud imperial powers give way,
   And at the cause bewail.

Along the common tide,
   Pallid he floated with a hideous yell;
Napoleon bellowed at his side,
And saw compassion all denied;
Beneath his stroke, ten thousand died,
   And wounded millions fell.

Ye breathe a doleful strain,
   Pursued at once by heavy rending peals;
He heaved his thunders from the main,
In purple gore he dyed the plain,
Then boasted his legions slain,
   Beneath the ruthless wheel.

Pregnant with every ill,
   He breathed his stenched diseases from afar;
A quiet world no more was still,
And terrors broke from hill to hill,
Whose bloody thirst was all to kill,
   Which stood before his car.

THE HAPPY BIRD'S NEST.

When on my cottage falls the placid shower,
   When evening calls the laborer home to rest;
When glad the bee deserts the hermid flower,
   O, then the bird assumes her peaceful nest.

When sable shadows grow unshapely tall,
   And sol's resplendant wheel descends the west,
The knell of respiration tolls for all,
   And Hesper smiles upon the linnet's nest.

When o'er the mountain bounds the fair gazelle,
   The night bird tells her day departing jest,
She gladly leaves her melancholy dell,
   And spreads her pinions o'er the linnet's nest.

Then harmless dean spreads her lucid sail,
   And glides through ether with her silver crest;
Bidding the watchful bird still pour her tale,
   And cheer the happy linnet in her nest.

Thus may some guardian angel bear her light,
   And o'er thy tomb departed genius rest;
Whilst thou shalt take thy long eternal flight,
   And leave some faithful bird to guard thy nest.

THE FATE OF AN INNOCENT DOG.

When Tiger left his native yard,
He did not many ills regard,

A fleet and harmless cur;
Indeed he was a trusty dog,
And did not through the pasture prog,
The grazing flock to stir, poor dog.
   The grazing flocks to stir.

He through a field by chance was led
In quest of game, not far ahead,
   And made one active leap,
When all at once, alarmed, he espied
A creature weltering on its side,
A deadly wounded sheep, alas!
   A deadly wounded sheep.

He there was filled with sudden fear,
Apprised of lurking danger near,
   And there he left his trail;
Indeed, he was afraid to yelp,
Nor could he grant the creature help,
But wheeled and dropped his tail, poor dog,
   But wheeled and dropped his tail.

It was his pastime, pride and fun,
At morn the nimble hare to run,
   When frost was on the grass;
Returning home, who should he meet,
The wether's owner coming fleet,
Who scorned to let him pass, alas!
   Who scorned to let him pass.

Tiger could but his bristles raise,
A surly complement he pays,
   Insulted shows his wrath,
Returns a just defensive growl,
And does not turn aside to prowl,
But onward keeps the path, poor dog!
   But onward keeps the path.

The raging owner found the brute,
But could afford no recruit,
  Nor raise it up to stand;
'Twas mangled by some other dogs,
A set of detrimental rogues,
Raised up at no command, alas!
  Raised up at no command.

Sagacious tiger left his bogs,
But lure the blame of other dogs,
  With powder, fire and ball;
They killed the poor unlawful game,
And then came back and eat the same,
But tiger paid for all, poor dog,
  But tiger paid for all.

Let every harmless dog beware
Lest he be taken in the snare;
  And scorn such fields to roam,
A creature may be frought with grace,
And suffer for the vile and base,
By straggling off from home, alas!
  By straggling off from home.

The blood of creatures oft is spilt,
Who die without a shade of guilt—
  Look out or cease to roam—
Whilst up and down the world he plays,
For pleasure, man, in danger strays
Without a friend from home, alas!
  Without a friend from home.

THE TIPPLER TO HIS BOTTLE.

What hast thou ever done for me?
  Defeated every good endeavor,
I never can through life agree
To place my confidence in thee,
    No, never! no, never!

Often have I thy stream admired,
  Thou nothing hast availed me ever,
Vain have I thought myself inspired;
Say have I else but pain acquired?
    Not ever! no, never!

No earthly good, no stream of health,
  Flows from thy fount thou cheerful giver,
From thee affluence sinks to stealth,
From thee I pluck no bloom of health,
    Whatever! no, never!

Thou canst impart a noble mind,
  Power from my tongue flows like a river,
The gas flows dead I'm left behind,
To all that's evil down conjured,
    To flourish more, never!

With thee I must thro' life complain,
  Thy powers at large will union sever,
Disgorge no more thy killing bane,
The bird, hope, flies from thee in vain,
    To return more, never!

ROSABELLA—PURITY OF HEART.

Though with an angel's tongue,
  I set on fire the congregations all,
'Tis but a brazen bell that I have rung,
  And I to nothing fall,
My theme is but an idle air,
If Rosabella is not there.

Though I in thunders rave,
  And hurl the blaze of oratoric flowers,
Others I move but fail myself to save,
  With my declaiming powers,
I sink, alas! I know not where,
If Rosabella is not there.

Though I point out the way,
  And closely circumscribe the path to Heaven,
And pour my melting prayer without delay,
  And vow my sins forgiven,
I sink into the gloom, despair,
If Rosabella is not there.

Though I may mountains move,
  And make the valleys vocal with my song,
I'm vain without a stream of mystic love,
  For all my heart is wrung,
I've laid myself a cruel snare,
If Rosabella is not there.

From bibliothic stores
  I fly proclaiming Heaven from land to land,
Or cross the seas and reach their distant shores,
  'Mid gothic groups to stand,
O, let me of myself beware,
If Rosabella is not there.

Our classic books must fail,
   And with their flow'ry tongue's to ashes burn,
And not one groat a mortal wit bewail,
   Upon his last return,
Be this the creature's faithful prayer,
That Rosabella may be there.

This spotless maid was born,
   The babe of Heaven and cannot be defiled,
The soul is dead and in a state forlorn,
   On which she has not smiled,
Vain are the circle and the fair,
If Rosabella be not there.

When other pleasures tire,
   And mortal glories fade to glow no more,
She with the wing of truth augments her fire,
   And still prevails to soar,
All else must die the good and wise,
But Rosabella never dies.

FALSE WEIGHT.

If thou art fair, deal lady fair,
   And let the scales be even;
Forbid the prising beam to rear,
   And pull thee down from Heaven.

Dost thou desire to die in peace,
   For every sin forgiven;
Give back my right, my weight decrease,
   And mount like mine to Heaven.

Rather give over to the poor,
    Take ten and give eleven;
Or else be fair, I ask no more,
    'Tis all required of Heaven.

And when on thee for pay I call,
    Which is but four for seven;
Keep nothing back, but pay it all,
    It is not hid from Heaven.

Remember hence, the sentence past,
    The truth in Scriptures given;
Last shall be first, and first be last,
    In time, in earth and Heaven.

DEPARTING SUMMER.

When auburn autumn mounts the stage,
    And summer fails her charms to yield;
Bleak nature turns another page,
    To light the glories of the field.

At once the vale declines to bloom,
    The forest smiles no longer gay;
Gardens are left without perfume,
    The rose and lilly pine away.

The orchard bows her fruitless head,
    As one divested of her store;
Or, like a queen whose train has fled,
    And left her sad to smile no more.

That bird which breath'd her vernal song,
    And hopp'd along the flow'ry spray ;
Now silent holds her warbling tongue,
    Which dulcifies the feast of May.

But let each bitter have its sweet;
    No change of nature is in vain ;
'Tis just, alternate, cold and heat,
    For time pleasure mixed with pain.

REFLECTIONS FROM THE FLASH OF A METEOR.

Psalm X, 12.

So teach me to regard my day,
    How small a point my life appears;
One gleam to death the whole betrays,
    A momentary flash of years.

One moment smiles, the scene is past,
    Life's gaudy bloom at once we shed ;
And sink beneath affliction's blast,
    Or drop as soon among the dead.

Short is the chain wound up at morn,
    Which oft runs down and stops at noon ;
Thus in a moment man is born,
    And lo ! the creature dies as soon.

Life's little torch, how soon forgot,
    Dim burning on its dreary shore ;
Just like that star which downward shot,
    It glimmers and is seen no more.

Teach me to draw this transient breath,
   With conscious awe my end to prove;
Early to make my peace with death,
   And thus in haste from time we move.

O Heaven, thro' this murky vale,
   Direct me with a burning pen;
Thus shall I, on a tuneful gale,
   Fleet on my three score years and ten.

TRUE FRIENDSHIP.

Friendship! thou balm of every ill,
   I must aspire to thee,
Whose breezes bid the heart be still,
And render sweet the patient's pill,
   And set the prisoner free.

Friendship! it is the softest soul
   Which feels another's pain,
And must with equal sighs condole,
While sympathetic streamlets roll,
   Which nothing can restrain.

Not to be nominated smart,
   Of mortals to be seen,
She does not thus her gifts impart,
Her aid is from a feeling heart—
   A principle within.

When the stranger, forced to roam,
   Comes shiv'ring to her door,
At once he finds a welcome home,
The torch of grace dispels the gloom,
   And bids him grope no more.

Friendship was never known to fail,
   The voice of need to hear,
When ruthless ills our peace assail,
When from our heart she draws the veil,
   And dry's the falling tear.

When dogs and devils snarl and fight,
   She hides and dwells alone,
When friends and kindred disunite,
With pity she surveys the sight,
   And gives to each his own.

Friendship has not a sister grace,
   Her wonders to exceed,
She is the queen of all her race,
Whose charms the stoutest must embrace,
   When in the vale of need.

Friendship is but the feeling sigh,
   The sympathising tear,
Constrained to flow till others dry,
Nor let the needy soul pass by,
   Nor scorn to see or hear.

ON THE CONVERSION OF A SISTER.

'Tis the voice of my sister at home,
   Resigned to the treasure above,
Inviting the strangers to come
   And feast at the banquet of love.

'Tis a spirit cut loose from its chains,
   'Tis the voice of a culprit forgiven,
Restored from a prison of pains
   With the sound of a concert from Heaven.

'T is a beam from the regions of light,
    A torch of beatific fire,
A spirit exulting for flight,
    With a strong and impatient desire.

'T is a drop from the ocean of love,
    A foretaste of pleasure to come,
Distill'd from the fountain above,
    The joy which awaits her at home.

EARLY AFFECTION.

I lov'd thee from the earliest dawn,
    When first I saw thy beauty's ray,
And will, until life's eve comes on,
    And beauty's blossom fades away;
And when all things go well with thee,
With smiles and tears remember me.

I 'll love thee when thy morn is past,
    And wheedling gallantry is o'er,
When youth is lost in ages blast,
    And beauty can ascend no more,
And when life's journey ends with thee,
O, then look back and think of me.

I 'll love thee with a smile or frown,
    'Mid sorrow's gloom or pleasure's light,
And when the chain of life runs down,
    Pursue thy last eternal flight,
When thou hast spread thy wing to flee,
Still, still, a moment wait for me.

I 'll love thee for those sparkling eyes,
   To which my fondness was betray'd,
Bearing the tincture of the skies,
   To glow when other beauties fade,
And when they sink too low to see,
Reflect an azure beam on me.

CONNUBIAL FELICITY.

The fairest soonest fade,
Young brides in flowers array'd,
   Will soon grow old,
   And prove a scold,
Tho' their forms decay'd.

But would you live with her at ease,
   Fly from the elf and leave her,
The only means a dame to please,
   Is by your flight to grieve her.

The sweetest soonest pall,
The tallest soonest fall,
   The tender bloom,
   Of sweet perfume,
Will pine the first of all.

Little regard the ills of life,
   Her frowns are but to flatter,
So when your flight has grieved your w
   Come back and discord scatter.

The gaudy charms of May,
Are quickly past away,
   The honey moon,
   Will change as soon,
And love to ills betray.

The fairest fruit upon the tree,
   Is ever soonest rotten,
Know in as much the nuptial glee.
   Must pass and be forgotten.

NO, NEVER LOVE.

What, take thee for my wedded wife,
   Then with another fly and leave thee?
No, never, never during life,
   Have I the notion thus to grieve thee,
     Never love, no never!

For well I know it would be death,
   At once myself from thee to sever,
Like the eternal flight of breath,
   The mystic spirit gone forever,
     Never love, not ever!

O! dol'rous cause who ever heard,
   The sad, the melancholy story,
The tale of love's departing bird,
   When wedlock lost her torch of glory,
     Few ever love, few ever!

My husband leaves his native shore,
   Along the roaring breakers sweeping,
Alas! and to return no more,
   He leaves his love behind him weeping,
     With hopes all lost forever!

Projecting o'er the frantic sea,
  She gazes from a lofty mountain,
To have her soul from trouble flee,
  Consigns her body to the fountain,
    Resolv'd to die forever!

At once she makes her distant leap,
  And bids her friends to languish never,
But yells before she strikes the deep,
  And bids the world adieu forever,
    Forever and forever!

DISCARDED BY A FALSE SUITOR.

Go worthless reptile go,
  Thou spoiler of my daughter's charms,
Thy hidden bane shall sink thee low,
  With death wrapped in thine arms.

Thou shall not hence beguile,
  The silly nymph that loves the dear,
Alarming fondness with a smile,
  To fade beneath a tear.

On youth's expanded wings,
  My child for fancy soared above,
But soon she fell beneath the sting,
  Of unrequited love.

Thy torch thy false guide star,
  Take care may burn thee up at last,
Or lead astray thy feet afar,
  And pain thy pleasures blast.

RECOLLECTIONS OF PAST EVENTS.

'Tis sweetest when the night is gone,
  The substance of a pleasing dream,
  Awakes the most delightful theme,
When to one's self alone,
  Those pleasures only break in sight,
  Fresh with the streams of morning light.

The spring is sweetest after past,
  For wonders fail to charm before,
  O, then look back, the scene adore,
'Mid autumns deepest blast;
  Thus hoary age looks back in truth,
  And smiles upon the charms of youth.

No less delight the summer shows,
  Where surly winter takes her seat;
  She then and then alone is sweet,
For dreams her charms disclose:
  To shun the hidden ills be sure,
  Wait till the greener fruits mature.

Wedlock must long have past away,
  Before its charms can well be known,
  For often men their wives disown,
Till years their deeds display:
  The sweets of time can best be told,
  In after years when life is old.

Will not eternity be sweet,
  When dreaming nature sleeps no more,
  When the short night of time is o'er,
And world's in union meet—
  The mem'ry of pure deeds in time,
  Live in seraphic world's sublime.

THE INTEMPERANCE CLUB.

On smiling wealth, intemp'rance war began,
  Away young health and mother genius flew;
And when from the child and parent ran,
  In stepped Dyspepsia belching, how do ye do?

'Twas then the din of desperation rose,
  Pleasure and pain at once their daggers drew;
Pain with his rod struck pleasure on the nose—
  In stepped lean Palsy trembling, how do ye do?

Young health came back to take a peep,
  But stay'd not long the ghastly sight to view;
And on her flight could not forbear to weep—
  In stepped the Cholic frowning, how do ye do?

She heard the crash of gambling rend the floor,
  And in the house saw poverty's dull crew;
When down the foot of Bolus kicked the door—
  In stepped the King of Terrors, how do ye do?

JEFFERSON IN A TIGHT PLACE.

THE FOX IS CAUGHT.

The blood hounds, long upon the trail,
Have rambled faithful, hill and dale:
But mind, such creatures never fail,
  To run the rebel down.
His fears forbid him long to stop,
Altho' he gains the mountain top,
He soon is made his tail to drop,
  And fleets to leave the hounds.

Alas! he speeds from place to place,
Such is the fox upon the chase;
To him the mud is no disgrace,
  No lair his cause defends.
He leaves a law and seeks a dell,
And where to fly 'tis hard to tell;
He fears before to meet with hell,
  Behind he has no friends.

But who can pity such a fox,
Though buried among the rocks;
He's a nuisance among the flocks,
  And sucks the blood of geese.
He takes advantage of the sheep,
His nature is at night to creep,
And rob the flocks while the herdsmen sleep,
  When dogs can have no peace.

But he is now brought to a bay,
However fast he run away,
He knows he has not long to stay,
  And assumes a raccoon's dress.
Found in a hole, he veils his face,
And fain would take a lady's place,
But fails, for he has run his race,
  And falls into distress.

The fox is captured in his den,
The martial troops of Michigan,
May hence be known the fleetest men,
  For Davis is their prey.
Great Babylon has fallen down,
A King is left without a crown,
Stripped of honors and renown,
  The evening ends the day.

GEN. JORDAN, COMMANDING 1st BRIG., 3d CAV. DIV., CAV. CORPS, M. D. M.

Bold Jordan, tho' subordinate,
Merits his boon, tho' not so great,
   He was firm to his post;
'Mid battles teen, he braved the storm,
Resolv'd his duty to perform,
   What ever ills they cost.

True, he was prosperous on his way,
The deeds of valor to display,
   His soldiers to control;
He seemed regardless of the cloud,
Which teemed with rebel thunders loud,
   Which did with vengeance roll.

And can we live him out,
Who helped the cursed foe to route,
   And made him bend the knee;
He flourished in his martial cause,
And aided to confirm the laws,
   To set Columbia free.

Hurrah for Jordan, give him praise,
Ye vassals bask beneath the blaze,
   Of one who is your friend;
And others in the battle live,
Who fought and left you not to grieve,
   To whom all knees should bend.

THE SOLDIER ON HIS WAY HOME

Soon, soon we shall depart,
  Like light ascending out of gloom;
We now are ready to depart,
  To our dear native home.

Adieu, ye noisy drums,
  No more we hear dread monsters roar;
Adieu, ye thunder teeming guns,
  Ye shake our camp no more.

We surely must rejoice,
  We have no longer hence to roam;
Left like a trump, each joy prevail,
  We're on our journey home.

Home is the sweetest place,
  Who will not be contented there;
Rather than rove thro' woods apace,
  With sorrow, gloom and fear.

Sound a loud tap before,
  And let our kindred know we come,
Let voices like sweet thunder war,
  We soon shall land at home.

The fields in rich array,
  And streamlets bubling as they flow,
Allure the pensive mind away,
  Whilst vallies smile below.

We now anticipate,
  Our gardens teeming fresh in bloom,
And kindred meet us at the gate,
  Glad that we are at home.

THE SOLDIER AT HOME.

We now salute our long lost friends,
    And leave the conflict all behind;
Rejoice, the storm of rupture ends,
    To which we have been long confined.

Secelia yet retains her lyre,
    On which she long before has play'd;
Attentive vesto forms the fire,
And cheers me in the cloister shade.

Salute my gentle mother's hand,
    Which led me when a feeble child,
Where the lone oak and willow stand,
    On which I have so often smil'd.

Embrace our kindred in our arms,
    And say till death we part no more;
No hostile threats our hearts alarm,
    Go when Heaven calls and not before.

Ceres invites us to the plough,
    Or leads us thro' the glades of pan;
And calls at eve the teeming cow,
    Then let us stay at home who can.

Dost thou not hear that lucid star,
    Ascending gently as from gloom;
Leave not thy dear companions far,
    But live in peace with them at home,

Arise then from the pit of war,
    The battle's won, arise and bloom;
Once firm let nought thy system jar,
    But stand nor leave thy friends at home.

THE ANGEL OF DEATH AT THE BED OF A DYING SAINT.

Wilt thou from gasping swerve,
  Or dare my fatal torch deny;
Does not thy soul my smile deserve,
  Which bids its fabric die.

Hast thou not lived to prove,
  The aid I thee have given,
With beams of providential love,
  Which oft thy love has driven.

Have I not faithful dealt
  With thee, and heard thy plaint on earth:
And for thy deep distress felt,
  And turned thy grief to mirth.

Free let those schackles fall
  Which keep thee from thy native sky.
Which binds thee to this loathsome ball,
  And bids thee grieve to die!

THE FLIGHT OF THOUGHT.

Say, what is there so wondrous as a thought,
  The ambient breezes seldom wander more;
It flies through unknown climes with wonder fraught,
  Creation to explore.

Far quicker than the vivid lightning flash,
  From Africa to Europe darts the mind,
It still continues on its wings apace,
  And leaves its cage behind.

Thought is a spirit, though within the brain,
   It steals away and yet we know not how;
Nothing confines it but to break its chain,
   Its stream remains to flow.

Thought in a moment leaps beyond the moon,
   Its mystic operation who shall know;
It bounds to Etherr, and darts back as soon
   Into its cage below.

The flight of thought is hard to comprehend,
   Just like the wind, it has no space of rest;
To traverse regions to its mighty end
   In North, South, East and West.

No mortal man can keep pace with the mind,
   Who hobbles as in fetters as he goes;
He thus remains within the flesh confined,
   At night in still repose.

Its rays extend through unknown empires far,
   Conspiring lines ne'er seen a fairer sight;
It fleets on rapid nymphs from star to star,
   Almost an infinite flight.

POVERTY.

Yes, poverty, though pining, yet must thrive,
She seems a creature dead, and yet alive;
She must, at large, herself with shame betray,
And frowning from herself would steal away.

But mind the rich in wealth is surely poor,
He gathers much, and yet he pines for more;
By discontent he makes his progress rough,
And never can suppose he has enough.

A life of poverty is for the best,
For thus at night a man may take his rest;
The author of his health he may adore,
And fails to pine, because he has no more.

Immortal virtue is the queen at last,
In poverty she lives, when wealth is past;
When mammon bloom has faded on the mind,
The stream of poverty becomes combined.

The cloudless mirror of the faultless soul
Reflects a pleasure which commands the whole;
One is considered poor when he is rich,
There is a destiny assigned to each.

A line of destiny for every good,
Received by all who ever there have stood;
Though I by poverty continue poor,
Let me the pain of poverty endure.

Dishonesty mounts high, but soon to fall,
Never to rise again at all, at all;
An overruling providence lifts up
The head of poverty when mammon stoops.

Exalted Babel with her blooming tower,
Fell sadly down in spite of all her power,
Hence, let all the proud and thrifty cease to boast
Of that which in a moment may be lost.

Gay fortune, let dull poverty alone,
Thy flower is withered and thy bird is flown.
Thou whom thy neighbors progress long delay,
Hast fallen low with all thy trust betray'd.

THE USE OF LIBERTY.

With liberty simply all nations are blest,
   To wander creation all over,
And toil for eternity there is their rest,
   The right of all things first discover;
But learn in the ramble yourself to control,
And strictly take care of both body and soul,
For peace with our Maker and law is the whole,
   The pride and the crown of a nation.

But man in a nation without a true wife,
   Had better continue without one,
To live in contention forever in strife,
   Why should I be crazy about one?
Whoever endeavors to keep one in pain,
Your liberty thus is wound up in a chain,
For why should one ever be free to complain,
   The disgust and mock of his nation?

But freedom is not what some take it to be,
   A boon which we never should trifle,
A man may be turned loose and find himself free,
   To ramble the woods with his rifle,
He oft leaves behind him a hut of disgrace,
Without a rough servant to dig in his place,
He's not calculated to prowl thro' the chase,
   But rather to rob his own nation.

Take care recent free men what you are about,
  You are not aware of your danger,
This never should make you too selfish and stout,
  Be never to business a stranger,
Be careful to gather what wisdom you can,
Acknowledge yourself to be only a man;
To undermine others avoid such a plan,
  And shine like a star in your nation.

Whatever your life's occupation may be,
  A teacher, a ploughman or student,
Be never too selfish because you are free,
  To learn in your course to be prudent,
The springs little streamlet must swell as it flows,
The more runs into it the larger it grows,
Till into the ocean a river it flows,
  And mingles the flood of a nation.

A man never should boast that he lives at his ease,
  Because he is free from his master,
Because I can ramble wherever I please ;
  At nothing I strive none the faster,
I have not a servant, I have not a horse,
And have not the power to take one by force,
If nothing to keep one it makes it still worse,
  And poverty takes the plantation.

EULOGY ON THE DEATH OF A SISTER.

Her sun of life is set,
  But still the vital stars of memory bloom,
The torch of fame has not extinguished yet,
  Still glimmering o'er the tomb ;
Be still my soul, but languish never,

Death but kills the pain,
    Welcome the knell,
    Fare thee well,
We soon shall meet again.

My sister was my friend,
   Who sought the distant smiles of brother love,
Whose pleasure was her safety to defend,
    And all her cares remove;
Be still my soul, indulge no sorrow,
   Death but kills the pain, &c.

Sister, farewell awhile,
   Encircled by a bright seraphic throng,
Thy tears will soon be turned into a smile,
   And weeping into song ;
Be still my soul, for joys await thee,
   Death only kills the pain,
    Welcome the knell,
    Farewell thee well,
We'll shortly meet again.

THE LATE THUNDER STORM WHILE IN CA. AT CONCORD, N. C., JUNE 20, 1865.

'T was like the peals on Sinai's hill,
When all the humble plains were still,
Which trembled from the thunder's voice,
Too dread for heathen to rejoice,
   But shudder at the sound ;
The lightning streaming from his eyes,
Rent as it broke through all the skies,
Its headlong course the world defies,
From which the affrighted creature flies,
   For shelter in the ground.

Out from his mouth went tones of death,
All nature kindled from his breath,
From land to land the rupture spread,
And bade all living creatures dread
   August Jehovah's ire;
Ye cedars of the mountain brake,
Ye summits reel, ye vallies shake,
Ye hidden beasts your dens forsake,
And ye who dare to sleep, awake
   From unextinguished fire.

From Teman thus Jehovah came,
And all the fields were wrapp'd in flame;
Thus did the world his wrath provoke;
The air was darkened with the smoke,
   Who can his wrath abide?
The leopard hastened to the rock,
Whilst every creature felt the shock,
'T was death among the grazing stock,
Astonished were the scattered flock,
   Which sought in vain to hide.

All ether seemed a fun'ral shroud,
The concave vaults were stern with cloud,
The lightenings leap, the thunders roll,
And earth seems rent from pole to pole,
   The mountains bowed beneath;
His nostrils breathed the livid stream,
The air was scorched before the flame;
The thunder acclimates the same,
Aloud to spread Jehovah's fame,
   And load the heavens with death.

McCROOM TO HIS MISS.

I do not want thee, flitting girl,
   I do not want thy hoops and laces,
For every self-applauding curl,
   A pensive thought disgraces.

I care not for thy flatt'ring hum,
   'T is but a syren to deceive me,
I 'd rather have one gill of rum
   Than all thou hast to give me.

And tho' thou hast my woos denied,
   Beware, it only was to try thee,
I do not languish for a bride,
   I also will deny thee.

I know thou hast no care for me,
   Thou wishest all the world to plunder,
Beware, I have as much for thee,
   I have the same to wander.

I'm willing, Miss, to bear the scorn,
   And be of thee denied forever,
For thee I cannot be forlorn,
   No! never, never, never!

ADVICE TO THE EXTRAVAGANT, PROUD AND IDLE.

There is a time for labor,
   There is a time to play,
To use the sword or sabre,
   And spurn the ills away.

Fools may try to detain you,
    But disregard the snare,
And let them not constrain you
    To leave a task so dear.

Then what is this in nature
    That constitutes a bliss?
We say to every creature,
    The truth lies but in this:
If you depend on giving,
    You will yourself deceive,
Or sacrifice your living,
    And bring yourself to grieve.

There is not one in twenty
    That e'er has much to spare,
Tho' he has moderate plenty;
    But stop the matter there;
Had you not play'd with folly,
    It might with you be well;
For now you might be jolly
    With corn and wheat to sell.

The sting of ev'ry evil,
    From idle chat came in,
Conversing with the devil,
    The base of every sin,
You miss the road to pleasure,
    And take the meaning wrong,
Or turn the word to leisure,
    And idly pass along.

Then do not pride in giving
    Your little mites away,
For friends destroy your living,
    But none your debts will pay;

You'd best not, tho' you love it,
　　Full tables to display,
For soon your friends will covet
　　Your living all away.

THE ART OF A POET.

True nature first inspires the man,
But he must after learn to scan,
　　And mark well every rule;
Gradual the climax then ascend,
And prove the contrast in the end,
　　Between the wit and fool.

A fool tho' blind, may write a verse,
And seem from folly to emerge,
　　And ryme well every line;
One lucky, void of light, may guess,
And safely to the point may press,
　　But this does not refine.

Polish mirror, clear to shine,
And streams must run if they refine,
　　And widen as they flow;
The diamonds water lies concealed,
Till polished it is ne'er revealed,
　　Its glory bright to show.

A bard must traverse o'er the world,
Where things concealed must rise unfurled,
　　And tread the foot of yore;
Tho' he may sweetly harp and sing,
But strictly prune the mental wing,
　　Before the mind can soar.

THE MAMMOTH.

Unknown majestic beast,
  Thy massive trace was found in ages past;
This we adopt, and do not doubt the least,
  Thy fame through time will last.

We credit this as truth—
  The trace of such a wondrous beast was found;
In by-gone years when time was in its youth,
  It traversed o'er the ground.

Stupendous elephant,
  Say not no form was made to equal thine;
Antiquity portrays the past event,
  For there he left the sign.

And thou enormous whale,
  Whose bulk surpasses all the water train,
With him to measure their attempts all fail,
  For thou wouldst swell in vain.

But this was far too vast,
  His magnitude was not announced as good,
And hence he was not suffered long to last,
  But was swept off by the flood.

ALEXANDER THE GREAT.

VAIN PRIDE.

From Pride's imperial mount,
  He cast his perspicacious eyes,
With schemes to wondrous to account;
He tries to swim the elysian fount,

But stabs himself and dies.
    No eye is given,
    Below the heaven,
To trace him where he flies.

Where is the sun of pride?
  Where has the bird of glory fled?
  His plume was bright, but soon was shed,
He flapped his wing and died;
    His schemes of old,
    Have not been told,
In vain the wits have tried.

His gaudy race is run,
  No more to boast his thousands slain,
  Nor ride the sanguinary plain,
And boast booty won;
    Thus in disgrace,
    He closed his race,
And sighed to beat the sun.

His fields in smiles arrayed,
  He knows no more, reposed in gloom;
  His bones are cloistered in the tomb,
With all his frame decayed;
    His conquering power,
    Forbears to tower,
To death and worms betray'd.

Where is the slaughtering great?
  His lambent banners now are furled,
  No more to subjugate the world,
And stalk in robes of state;
    The storm is still,
    No more to kill,
And peace is all complete.

REGRETTED PAST TIME.

Upwards my hand I lift,
  To seize a lambent blossom,
Whose glow-worm is a gift,
  To canker on my bosom,
No more of this away, away,
The charms of which life to ills betray,
  And dim our microcosm.

What is the vivid gleam,
  A light from fools we borrow,
To-day a transient dream,
  Which sinks in gloom to-morrow,
Ye flitting belles adieu, adieu,
I cannot spend the day with you,
  Whose sun goes down in sorrow.

Come down from pleasure's throne,
  Whose lights but darkly glimmer,
Tho' up they high were blown,
  But now, alas! grow dimmer,
Let me sweet virtue's fields explore,
No more of this, no more, no more,
  Which keeps life in a tremor.

Adieu my fair gazelle,
  Thou hast no lasting treasure,
No more fond tales I tell,
  To gain at twilight pleasure,
Pleasure is gone I know not where,
Not ever true if ever here,
  If so but short the measure.

High, high, the buck may mount,
  But falls as soon forever,
What is the next account?
  He fell his bones to shiver,
And hence it floats upon the gale,
The buck left nothing but his tail,
  Which fell his neck to sever.

THE HERMIT'S VIEW FROM THE MOUNTAIN.

When I stood on the top of the mountain,
And gazed from its heights to the fountain,
The wonder was far fast recounting,
  My language would fail me to tell;
Astonished the hermit stood trembling,
From fish in the water assembling,
He feared he should down travel, tumbling,
  Deep in the dark abyss to dwell.

The beautiful swan cackled loving,
With her wings round the rush covert waving
An aspect almost past engraving,
  What wonders can nature display;
The limners of great imitation,
Would sink in wild imagination,
And ramble through all the creation,
  And never this wonder portray.

The aspect of old yellow Tiber,
Compared to this is but a fibre,
Perhaps not a mortal discriber,
  Can paint out its equal in time;

BY HORTON.

The water meandered in wonder,
Constrained he looked up and then under,
His mind through the vission must blunde
　Thro' nature profound and sublime.

The prospect surpassed the vast ocean,
Eternally heaving in motion,
Some think that it is but an ocean,
　To strike at the romantic scene;
Naught but to an angel in heaven,
Such noble descriptions are given,
Or the great one immortal in seven,
　The mortal has never yet been.

SONG OF LIBERTY.

The glorious plan of liberation,
　Opens now, a scene of joy
Roles spontaneous thro' the nation,
　Which no treason can destroy;
　　Lift all voices,
　All the world the theme employ.

Swell the peon, sing victorious,
　Storms subsided, leave a peace;
Liberation, O! how glorious,
　Start in numbers, not cease;
　　Send the shower down,
　And the shower shall increase.

Lift on high ten thousand voices,
　Blow the trump of Jubilee;
All the slavish land rejoices,
　Sing triumphant all are free;
　　Sing delightful,
　All who live this day to see.

Dart yo angels down from glory,
   Let your anthems blend with ours;
Freedom is a joyful story,
   Raise in songs selectial showers,
     As in Eden,
   Cluster in elysian bowers.

SHE AVERED SHE KNEW NOT WHAT TO SING

Sing of the hours when time was young,
   And life without a pain;
When music flowed from every tongue,
And sweetly through creation rung,
   And bade Jehovah reign.

Sing of the maids in Enna's field,
   When flowers were all divine;
And did in smile their pleasures yield,
When nothing lovely lay concealed,
   From charming proser fine.

Sing too of Phillip's martial son,
   Or Alexander's feast;
When his triumphant race was run,
The shaft of love was hard to shun,
   Which struck both man and beast.

Sing of the time when David, King,
   Subdued an envious Saul;
Who was constrained to dance and sin,
Whose violin rung from every string,
   And pleasure crowned the hall.

THE EYE DROP.

What but a tear could sorrow tell,
   Down stealing from the humid eye,
When like a crystal drop it fell,
   To ache the heart that heaves the sigh.

It slept upon her speechless tongue,
   But silence showed her feeling clear,
Till from her eyes the language sprung,
   The tale of sorrow was a tear.

'Twas like a deep and swelling flood,
   Which thro' a fissure breaks its way,
'Twas love which bursted with its load,
   The grief of parting to betray.

The tongue may utter fare thee well,
   And ev'ry sigh a friend endear,
But nothing has the power to tell,
   The heart's affection like a tear.

When friendship takes its flight away,
   No more forever to appear,
My tongue be still, but let me pay,
   The last fond tribute of a tear.

Ah! thus our feelings is betray'd,
   The sense of sorrow too severe,
It must the inmost powers pervade,
   And nothing shows it like a tear.

TOUCH NOT, HANDLE NOT, TASTE NOT.

If I handle I must touch,
  Tho' the deed be seeming small,
Every little calls as much,
  Then I must not touch at all.

If I taste a morsel sweet,
  Appetite will covet more,
Thus I shall myself defeat,
  Twenty craves another score.

Handle not the unclean thing,
  Let the blushing rose alone,
Where the insect lurks to sting,
  Tho' she hums the sweetest tone.

Life without but death within,
  Never heals a wounded heart,
Beauty ends once through the skin,
  From the bloom at once depart.

When I take the smallest sip,
  Soon the bird of caution flies,
Self-defence breaks from my lips,
  Conscience faints and virtue dies.

You know your failure, touch but light,
  Says the father to the son ;
Soon a jug becomes a mite,
  Start and soon the deed is done.

Start a wheel once down the hill,
  Down to run it cannot fail,
Raise the gate and start the mill,
  Start the boat and spread the sail.

Let the stranger son alone,
  Start not till you prove the end,
Tinker rare with things unknown,
  And let caution be your friend.

Handle not the unclean thing,
  Touch not, taste not of the bane,
Lest too late you feel the sting,
  Lost in unabating pain.

TO THE FOURTH.

JULY 4TH, 1865.

To-day you make your choices,
Lift up your hearts and voices,
And every heart rejoices,
  On this triumphal day.

Now let the proclamation,
Break through the land and nation,
The trump of free salvation,
  Aloud the cause display.

Salvation is the sweetest song,
That ever broke from mortal tongue,
It fills the whole seraphic throng,
  Throughout the worlds above;
What more can please by land or sea,
Than that which sets the bond-man free,
Lift ev'ry hand, bend ev'ry knee,
  Swell every heart with love.

We solemn this should mention,
It is the Lord's invention,
To take the werld's attention,
  The sound of victory won;
The labor is at leisure,
'Tis pain turned into pleasure,
A shower of gold and treasure,
  Now falls below the sun.

To-day, July the 4th, proclaim
  The day of celebration,
It lifts into public fame,
  Demanding jubilation,
O, let the sun rise not to set,
And we remain where first we met,
Never for mortal to regret,
  A scene to last forever.

Aloud and for the cannon's roar,
The triumph of the Western shore,
Oppression's voice be heard no more,
  Hence to disturb us never.

Whig, democrat or tory,
Each heart beats high for glory,
The most delightful story,
  Is this of all the three;
The Union is our mother,
We hence should love each other,
The sister and the brother,
  Rejoice we all are free.

HARD IS THE SENTENCE OF PARTING MAN AND WIFE, THOUGH THEY MAY HAVE MUCH DISAGREED.

Go on, may the kind heavens chide thee,
   No longer the pain of my arm,
I wish not an ill to betide thee,
   Beware that I wish thee no harm.
If thou art gone and gone forever,
   Swiftly, swiftly move,
If again I see thee never,
   Fare thee well my love.

Tell me what on earth could move thee,
   Hence no more to dwell,
Can'st thou say I did not love thee?
   No! but truly well.
If thou art gone resolved to leave me,
   Through the world to rove,
Be sure it cannot fail to grieve thee,
   Fare thee well my love.

Oh! what's like a husband off starting,
   To look on his wife never more,
'Tis the soul and the body fast parted,
   Is his flight from his own native door.
Art thou hence inclined to leave me ever,
   Kiss my cheek and move,
If again I see thee never,
   Fare thee well my love.

Still 'tis hard to give thee over,
   And to be resigned,
Hence with thee no more to hover,
   Lonely, left behind.

But if I had known thee never,
  This I could approve,
Dear, if art gone forever,
  Fare thee well my love.

But if I am quite forsaken,
  I'll take this trouble for one part,
I thought but was truly mistaken,
  And sigh with a pain in my heart—
These last words my tears impel,
  Hence no more this dove,
Words, heart rending fare thee well,
  Fare thee well my love.

But if thou art bound to leave me,
  Call me no more thine,
Was thy aims first to deceive me,
  Thou art no more mine,
Hence expostulate no more,
  But to leave me sick and sore,
Let me die and then remove,
  Fare thee well my love.

A WIFE, A WIFE, A WIFE, ALL THE DIN IS WIFE—OH FIE! FIE! FIE!

Away with all this folly,
  Which burdens down my life,
Which leads to melancholy,
  And strikes the road of strife,
Some small regard for cheat she pays,
And cheats me all my remnant days.

Say not a wife is for the best,
   That robs one of his leisure,
Eager with one though fair to rest,
   Without one lasting pleasure,
Few pleasures true, she may afford,
But after, oh! take care good lord.

Fancy proclaims angelic bloom,
   Her charms abound with heaven,
A garden fraught with sweet perfume,
   At morning, noon and even,
Oh, life is thus to death betrayed,
A danger sprite in smiles arrayed.

If by a woman life is crowned,
   She makes man's life a heaven,
That woman has not yet been found,
   One thousand sure, not seven,
If celibacy breeds concern,
Oh, try the good, the evil learn—
                  With sorrow!

BEWARE! I AM GONE!

Farwell to thee connubial flower,
   Whom 'twas my fate to wed,
And leave thee in thy native bower,
   Rosella, thou art dead.

Thy heart is far too hard to melt,
   I now myself conceal,
What is a heart that never felt,
   And yet too hard to feel.

Take thought, thy needless follies own,
   Thy burden on thy head,
Good bye! thy friend is out and gone,
   Rosella thou art dead.

Once we could talk together sweet,
   Each other could adore,
No more our follies to repeat,
   Together now no more.

Then let the time with pleasure fly,
   I have no tears to shed,
Good bye! it is in vain to cry,
   Rosella thou art dead.

THE POWER OF LOVE.

SHE SAID TO HER LOVER, I AM TOO YOUNG TO LO.

Oh tell me not thou art too young
   My eager question to approve;
The language of my heart and tongue,
   Which flows from love.

Thou art my choice, thou knowest well,
   Witness the truth ye heavens above;
The eye, without a tongue, can tell
   The tale of love.

Why wilt thou live a useless nun!
   For whom with brambles I would go;
Rather be with the dead than one
   Who cannot love.

From thee my morning pleasures rove
　With all the softness of a dove ;
But fear my eager suit will clove
　Without thy love.

THE HORSE STOLEN FROM THE CAMP.

He's gone, alas! I know not whither,
With hair and bones and flesh together ;
By hungry fowls he may be slain,
Hence, he will not come back again.

He's gone, but who can show his rider ?
Or if concealed, who knows his hider ?
One thing is sure, his tramps are o'er,
And hence, will here come back no more !

He's gone, and may be far the better,
As well as mine, the devil's debtor ;
He's gone, the buzzard's to deprive,
Who could not take the beast alive.

He's gone, but left no trace behind him,
And hence it will be hard to find him ;
If thee no more I'll ride old friend,
My good old pony, fare-thee-well !

WEEP.

Weep for the country in its present state,
And of the gloom which still the future wait ;
The proud confederate eagle heard the sound,
And with her flight fell prostrate to the ground !

Weep for the loss the country has sustained,
By which her now depedent is in jail;
The grief of him who now the war survived,
The conscript husbands and the weeping wives!

Weep for the seas of blood the battle cost,
And souls that ever hope forever lost!
The ravage of the field with no recruit,
Trees by vengeance blasted to the root!

Weep for the downfall o'er your heads and chief,
Who sunk without a medium of relief;
Who fell beneath the hatchet of their pride,
Then like the serpent bit themselves and died!

Weep for the downfall of your president,
Who far too late his folly must repent;
Who like the dragon did all heaven assail,
And dragged his friends to limbo with his tail!

Weep o'er peculiar swelling coffers void,
Our treasures left, and all their banks destroyed;
Their foundless notes replete with shame to all,
Expecting every day their final fall,
In quest of profit never to be won,
Then sadly fallen and forever down!

NEGRO SPECULATION.

We think of the shackles and fetters,
   And traverse to countries of pain;
'Tis written in blood-dripping letters,
   Whilst struggling, but fast in the chain!
      Weep humanity, weep!

Oh! where is my sister and brother?
 Gone, hopeless, the land to explore;
And, stationed afar from each other,
 To see their dear kindred no more!
  Weep humanity, weep.

Without a small breeze to revive them,
 They toiled in the sun-melting dell,
With rock-hearted tyrants to drive them,
 And nature is turned into hell!
  Weep humanity, weep!

He is by no pity defended
 Beneath the tyranical wave,
His life in a few days is ended,
 He's dragged to a premature grave!
  Weep humanity, weep!

THE PLEASURES OF FREE GRACE AND AN ANXIETY FOR A VIEW OF HEAVEN.

To the heavenly vision
 Immortal fruition I'd flee,
  And bathe in the seas of charming free grace,
 When shall I see—when shall I see—
  That happy place!

The stream from the fountain
 Rolls out to the mountain most free,
  And pearls in sweet water the song of free grace,
 When shall I see—when shall I see—
  That happy place!

One beam from its glory
  Would bring the sweet story to me,
    And teach me to lift the voice of free grace,
  When shall I see—when shall I see—
    That happy place?

To bring a sweet shower
  Fly glorious hour, bless day,
    And sin shall desert the reign of free grace,
  When shall I see—when shall I see—
    That happy place?

Oh! what is like heaven?
  One spirit in seven or three,
    Too pure to be seen by creatures so base,
  When shall I see—when shall I see—
    That happy place?

THE CHEERLESS CONDITION OF BACHELORSHIP

When Adam dwelt in Eden's shades alone,
He breathed to heaven a sad and piteous tone;
For nothing pleasing yet the world displayed,
Though he the blooming garden well surveyed.

Throughout the place no pleasing sound he heard,
No lovely scene unto his eye appeared;
Lone man was then a hermit, quite retired,
Whose flowery cot no cupid had inspired.

His Maker said he is not well alone,
Hence from his side I will extract a bone;
But an etheral opiate, sound and deep,
Man on his side was prostrate laid asleep.

Fresh to his view the smiling vision rose,
The queen of pleasure in his calm repose;
He woke in wonder from his pleasing dream,
To sing and tell it to the limpid stream.

When lo! he saw the bridal vision rise,
On whom he gazed with rapture and surprise;
Her charm was heaven, her visage glowed with love,
Whose smiles reflected grace thro' all the grove;
Thus did her glory crown the martial bower,
The rosy maid and queen of every flower.

The birds of Hymen struck the wondrous song,
And fragant breezes flowed with peace along;
Myriads of beasts flocked to their festive place,
Which pranced and bellowed round the scene of grace.

Then Philomena tune her lyric tongue,
And rung all night the hymenial song;
Such is the happy change of single life,
And such the pain of man without a wife;
No smiling dame his pleasures to divide,
A perfect stranger to a loving bride.

Nay, man alone is but a frantic elf,
A troubled sea, a burden to himself;
Without the knowledge of connubial bliss,
And what is life in such a state as this.

Melancholy wile, the stormy night,
The fluctuating vessel never right;
A clouded sky, a dull and sunless day,
A week which passes void of rest away.

Man strikes the road of fortune in his youth,
Which quickly ends, but seldom ends in truth;
Upon her plume he first directs his eyes,
Which lightly plays, but far before him flies;
Which, when he gains is withered by the blast,
And all his fond design is lost at last.

Mistaken man, the dearest gem is love,
The diamond which forbids the mind to rove;
The pride of nature, or the soothing wife,
The soul of pleasure, and the palm of life.

THE THOUGHT OF HOME IN BATTLE.

However distant still I love thee,
   However far away I roam,
'Tis my pleasure now to move thee,
   On my journey home.

The thought of thee makes still the crash,
   The trees in winter bloom,
I thought of thee at every flash,
   My dear native home.

While I was fighting far away,
   And fancied death my doom,
Still hope with thee, the brightest ray,
   The thought and love of home.

Tho' lightning flash and thunder roar,
   Or brackest ocean foam,
Still on the wing of hope I soar,
   And smile to think of home.

BY HORTON.

I bid thee once and long farewell,
  Far, far away to roam,
But now with joy can smiling tell,
  I'm on my journey home.

THE MEMORY OF A LADY IN BATTLE.

However thou art far away,
Memory reflects at twilight ray,
  Tho' thou art left behind,
And though I plough the deep wide sea,
Amid the waves I think of thee,
  The star upon my mind.

Oh! yes thou art mine only star,
A memory glimmering from afar,
  'Tis sad from thee to rove,
I never, never shall forget,
Thy grace, life's last sun shall set,
  For nothing darkens love.

But hence I trust to love no more,
This world of danger to explore,
  Beneath the heavens above,
However loud the peals of war,
I never shall forget my star,
  The torch of distant love.

THE FRIENDS LEFT AT HOME.

Think not that I am gone away,
   For me indulge no sorrow,
However far I go to-day,
   I may come back to-morrow.

And tho' I leave thee with a tear,
   Beware, 'tis not forever,
I must return to friends so dear,
   To leave more, never, never.

Mother, beware, I love thee yet,
   Wherever be my station,
I never shall my call regret,
   Because I love my nation.

But now I must forbear to roam,
   It is a pleasing story,
I smile and go exulting home,
   And seize my native glory.

No more to say friends all farewell,
   Nor leave them sadly weeping,
I come a better tale to tell,
   O'er hills and mountains leaping.

THE SOLDIER'S DISMISSAL.

It seems it is a joyful sound,
That flows the noisy camp around,
Like dead bones summons from the tomb,
The trump that calls the soldier home.

I hear my mother's lovely voice,
The message makes my heart rejoice,
Methinks I hear my father say,
Arise my son and come away.

Then listen to the general call,
A pleasing sound for one and all,
Its sound forever seems to roam,
The trumpet calls the soldier home.

Sons of Columbia learn the song,
The symphony of every tongue,
Resuscitate the soldier's heart,
And bid him from the camp depart.

Return, rejoicing as you go,
And bid adieu. to every foe,
Fields, gardens, orchards all in bloom,
Welcome the weary soldier home.

The purling brook methinks I hear,
Salute the approaching soldier's ear,
The pink, the lily and the rose,
Each to my view their charms disclose

And let us hence forbear to fight,
Ye soldiers wheel from left to right,
Accord in sound from every drum,
The trump that calls the soldier home.

DAVIS' FLIGHT.

The dragoon with his burning tail,
   Has gone forever out of sight;
And lift not one behind the wail,
   But rather triumph at his flight.
      Oh! blundering Davis go.

He is the wretch of all the earth,
   Who led the rebels thus away;
Who gave to gloomy plunder birth,
   Then run himself far, far away;
      Oh! blundering Davis go.

And now he's gone to Mexico,
   We think not long he there will dwell;
We are aware he next will go,
   To lodge with equal fools in hell;
      Oh! blundering Davis go.

Go drop thy plunder where thou wilt,
   In some deep pit or gloomy dell;
Thou canst not shun the shaft of guilt,
   Nor screen the thunderbolts of heaven;
      Go, go, forever go.

AFTER HIS DEPARTURE.

She hid every plate, spoon and knife,
   Refusing his bounty to see;
His pleasure was pain to her life,
   What kind of a lady was she?

Oh heaven! why had I not known,
  The gloom of my destiny first;
To be thus sequestered alone,
  Deserted, eternally curst.

Insane, she discovered his track,
  Though he had deserted and gone;
And as from a ghost recoiled back,
  To weep in her chamber alone.

'Twere better to know he was dead,
  In eternity's ocean to lay;
I should be more content in my bed,
  To know he was lodged is his grave.

Sigh for his presence in vain,
  'Tis terror wherever I move;
Sure nothing can equal the pain,
  Of one when deserted in love.

His fortune has finished my fate,
  Why had not some other been born;
A woman to put in my stead,
  I had not been weeping forlorn.

Why had I the progress began,
  With one who was destined to rove;
Why did I start off with the man,
  Who pays no attention to love.

Lone forest, thy branches so wide,
  With all thy sweet foliage of green;
My progress of life to decide,
  By mortal no more to be seen.

Let me plunge into some dark abyss,
    Afar from all nature removed ;
And hide from a cavern like this,
    A stranger to distressed love.

True I was his idol in life,
    But still was a pitiful prey ;
And never endeared as a wife,
    From whom he went careless away.

FAREWELL! FAREWELL!!

Farewell, I leave thee with regret,
    Without a moment to delay ;
Just like the sun rose to set,
    And close the busy scene of day.

Farewell, oh yes, the deep concern,
    Gives birth to many a falling tear ;
When parting never to return,
    Again to those he loved so dear.

Farewell, it pains the dripping eye,
    That never shed a tear before ;
It wakes the dormant sleeping sigh,
    To say that we shall meet no more.

Too well I know the pang of love,
    To smile and hear the parting knell ;
It turns a vulture to a dove,
    To say forever, fare thee well.

Then friend adieu, if sure we part,
   It is a bitter tale to tell;
A peal that breaks the tender heart,
   Now and forever, fare the well.

PEACE AT HOME.

'Tis when a storm subsides,
   And breathes a clement breeze behind,
   Such is the quiet stream of mind,
   Thus all things are to heaven resigned,
And friend with friend divides.

When peace is gone from home,
   A whirlwind resides in her stead,
   And all the laurel's leaves are shed,
   The willow droops her verdant head,
The chamber is a tomb.

Where peace forbears to dwell,
   Life from the hut or fleet away,
   Whose wife is pouting night or day,
   Oh, tortured man forbear to stay,
Her path leads unto hell.

A forward wife is death,
   Woman indeed is hard to find,
   Man to her end is ever blind,
   'Tis best to leave the wretch behind,
Nor spend with such a breath.

Why should one live on thorns,
  And yet a transient time to live,
  With one who will not take nor give,
  But will the dearest friend deceive,
And every favor scorn.

How pleasing is the hour,
  When a rude storm has passed away,
  And left the field and garden gay,
  Whilst lambent o'er the breast of May,
Play inoffensive flowers.

Never regret the flight,
  From one in her own folly left,
  Who frowns and tramples on a gift,
  Leave her alone herself to shift,
And vanish from her sight.

MY NATIVE HOME.

Oh! liberty my native land,
  From thee how can I bear to roam,
Or leave thy patriotic band,
  A stranger to my native home.

The distant isles aspire to thee,
  And plough the ocean's brackish foam,
A land from despotism free,
  My birthright and my native home.

No, let me die upon thy shore,
  And freedom flourish o'er my tomb,
Heaven grant me seraph's wings to soar,
  And leave in peace my native home.

Should I sail to some distant plain,
   Where pleasures laurels fail to bloom,
Oh! fortune o'er the stormy main,
   Back waft me to my native home.

Tho' gold and pearls abundant shine,
   And fortune crown the flowery dome,
But fair Columbia thou art mine,
   The lot of peace my native home.

When smoke from mortars vein the sky,
   With thunders from the shattering bomb,
Oh! let me then with safety fly,
   For shelter to my native home.

Let this be chased in my breast,
   Through this and future years to come,
My last abode, my final rest,
   Be lodged with thee my native home.

NEW FASHIONS.

There was a time when death was terror,
   Something harsh in every ear,
The tear left on the cheek a furrow,
   And every breath was drawn with fear;
Now the pall soon dies away,
Bury the dead and all be gay.

There was a time 'twas rare to marry,
   Wedding was a strange delight,
And the bride became a fairy,
   And the bridegroom an oddly sight;
Now the comic scenes are o'er,
And wedding flows from door to door.

There was a time that rare was danger,
    Dirks and pistols slept profound,
Thus sustain the harmless stranger,
    And the peasant was renowned;
Now all cry take care cut throat,
Long moustaches, caps and boots.

There was a time when rules were riches,
    Wives and husbands knew their own,
Women seldom wore the breeches,
    Left their husbands' ploughs alone;
Now tobacco rules have crossed,
And no one knows which chaws the most.

There was a time when peace was plenty,
    All the world could harmonize,
Few complained not one in twenty,
    Of good peas and pumpkin pies;
Soda shortens now the meal,
Else you'll hear a dreadful peal.

There was a time when debts were paid up,
    Money was not then to make,
Nor for distant fortune laid up,
    Down the credit or the break;
Now insolvent pleas are made,
Take once the oath the debt is paid.

There was a time when health was nourished,
    And brandy was not but a name,
Thrifty men by labor flourished,
    And prudence mounted into fame;
Now large drinks all health oppose,
Man drinks awhile and down he goes.

There was a time when ladies swore not,
   Teasing their husbands for a dram,
Draughts of gin their bosoms bore not,
   Effusing from their lips a damn ;
Now they swear, they drink and boast,
And the fairest drink the most.

There was a time when girls were fearful,
   Slow and backward truly proud,
Men in conversation careful,
   True they laughed but seldom loud ;
Now their fear they all have left,
And they solicit far the most.

ASPIRING HOME.

Oh blessed habitation, my only concern,
I'd fly home rejoicing, nor thence to return ;
   As an angel of glory,
   I'd tell a sweet story,
No longer thro' deserts so distant to roam ;
   My every endeavor,
   I'd dwell there forever,
For there is no place in the Union like home.

I'd say to my kindred friends how do you do,
I've traveled the countries and cities all thro'
   I was once melancholy,
   But now I am jolly,
I'll think of the fields and fair gardens in bloom ;
   No longer a stranger,
   Escaped from all danger,
Oh, what is so lov'd as my dear native home.

I cannot but think of my dear little wife,
The whole consolation and peace of my life;
    When from the tall mountain,
    I gaze on the fountain,
That stood near the seaside, loud hearing its foam;
    This thought was my pleasure,
    For she is my treasure,
The sole consolation and comfort of home.

The loud storms of battle my comfort assail,
And soldiers in crimson their comrades bewail;
    When trees split asunder,
    From cannons of thunder,
With mountains and valleys all shrouded in gloom;
    Oh what was my notion,
    What waves of emotion,
Oh heaven, I thought of my dear native home.

When climbing steep mountains o'er mantled with snow,
And icicles hung in the valleys below;
    O'er streams clearly glittered,
    With ice over fettered,
The summits resemble some wonderful dome;
    O'er hibernal evil,
    Back home let me travel,
Bare me back, waft me back to my dear native home.

FREEDOM.

    Man to be free must bear the axe,
    And every other tool he lacks;
    And if you wish to starve and fall,
    Throw by the mattock and the mawl.

If one for me has cut a path,
   And I prefer to take the woods;
I must incur from justice wrath,
   And folly leads from every good.

I soon am free and fall to play,
And just as soon I miss the way;
Poverty travels close behind,
And he becomes to pleasure blind.

Early he wants to take a wife,
   And that is nothing but a name;
As soon he enters into strife,
   Or early enters into shade.

Mark and let the wife alone,
And all you gain is but your own;
A humid woman bearing rule,
Is seldom better than a mule.

She's not what may be supposed,
For he has not her deeds disclosed;
'Tis she has gotten you by the hand,
To pull you at her own command.

If once a woman gets the start,
One or the other may depart;
For if with ease he drives the plow,
She soon will have him milk the cow.

You thus will find it far the best,
   To fix your plan before you wed;
Or else be ever robbed of rest,
   Whether without or in the bed.

Children will soon harth around,
  And every one demands his bread;
And nought or little will be found,
  To raise them almost from the dead.

Instead of rising free he's bound,
Cast by his freedom in the ground;
Brought by his idol down so low,
He's ashamed his head to show.

You'll find the word a bad mistake,
  We then the judge must deep reprove;
Set not your pleasure thus at stake,
  To marry first and work for love.

If you are free, be free indeed,
Be sure at home to take the lead;
Subdue your wife's destructive wave,
Nor let her bear you down a slave.

THE UNION OF PARTIES.

Like rivers in conflux, let parties now blend,
Who e'er was a foe, let him now be a friend;
In one tide of glory, together all mix,
The system of concord completely to fix;
  Let us all meet together, and all sing together—
                                            In the Union.

Like the union of heaven, the moon and the sun,
At times meet together, a short race to run;
Let us all run together, but not to divide,
That one in the other may safely confide;
  Let us all come together, and all sing together—
                                            In the Union.

Meet the lamb and the dove at the national bar,
No thunder of faction their system shall jar;
Like bright constellation in cluster to shine,
Fill the last crash of nature to flow and refine;
   Let us all walk together, and all sing together—
                             In the Union.

We'll mingle in wedlock, we'll mingle in prayer,
To interdict marriage what mortal shall dare;
No longer divided the nation shall be,
Let all go together, by land and by sea;
   Let us all go together, and all stick together—
                             In the Union.

How sweet is the union in heaven we see,
The planets in ether unwavering we see;
In this concentration, harmonious they move,
In wonderful concord, the union of love;
   Then we'll all walk togeher, and all sing together—
                             In the Union

SONG OF LIBERTY AND PARENTAL ADVICE.

   Come help me sing the morning song,
      While woods are sweetly blooming,
   And bears the joyful strain along,
      That happier days are coming.

   The gloom has left the light behind,
      With all the vassals shouting,
   We are no more in chains confined,
      And see the devil pouting.

Sing on, rejoicing not to cease,
  Regard no stint of money,
It now becomes a land of peace,
  To flow with milk and honey.

Sing on, be every man his own,
  It free who dare to perish?
Nor work your fingers to the bone,
  But work with ease and flourish.

Let other people's goods alone,
  But raise yourself a plenty;
To delve and cultivate your own,
  And beg not one in twenty.

How dare you touch another's spoil,
  When you have strength to labor?
Oh, then be glad to dig and toil,
  And let alone your neighbor.

Rather be able then to give,
  Than take their acquisition,
For care and puddles is to live,
  In competent condition.

We recommend to all good care,
  And keep all round you studying,
When health is good and weather fair,
  Your work will be quite cheering.

Your wife may well be busy too,
  Averting all starvation,
Keep clean herself, her house and you,
  And thus support her station.

Thus every man may live that way,
  Upon his own plantation,
Without the cost to steal or kill,
  But gladden his relation.

Close labor works you up to wealth,
  It makes your wife to love you;
If sick it oft restores to health,
  Tho' idlers may reprove you.

Thus did a man his son advise,
  Let not your friends deceive you,
If in the world you wish to rise,
  Take care of what I give you.

With fire but slightly touch good toe,
  It soon will blaze all over,
Thus prudent all things lively go,
  And all past loss recover.

Keep all your business right before,
  And clear up all around you,
Thus will they thrive and gather more,
  And nothing will confound you.

Ne'er think hard to bear your brunt,
  Your work will compensate you,
The knife of labor whet if blunt,
  And fortune will await you.

Another lesson you would give,
  Hold in your feet from rambling,
By straggling you can never live,
  By sporting nor by gambling.

Take not the bottle for your friend,
    For this will sure deceive you,
And this you may in truth depend,
    Both health and wealth will leave you.

It robs you of your rest at night,
    Take money fame and pleasure,
Which never can the loss requite,
    But drains the fount of pleasure.

SING ON.

Sing of the torch which set on fire,
    This cold inactive heart,
When love is eager to retire,
    Or on its wing depart;
Come back was whispered, oh come back,
Nor from my presence make one track!

Sing of the hours when I was young,
    The partner of a maid,
When loves like streams flowed from my tongue,
    Who had been long afraid;
Escort me timorous dandy come,
And bear the listening lady home!

Sing of the blooms which lambent played,
    O'er the fair garden's breast,
When fields were fresh in flowers arrayed,
    And noontide called to rest;
When round I heard the insect hum,
The woodbine and the fragrant gum.

Sing of the time when first I rose,
  Trembling for power to tell,
Nor dare the secret to disclose,
  To one beloved so well ;
Nor let one, lady, woo thee long,
Before I terminate my song.

AT LEAVING CAMP.

The ramping of the noisy camp,
  Beneath the sky serene ;
Like evening with a starlight lamp,
  It soon will close the scene.

These trees have dawned as free from blast,
  The turf we now pass o'er ;
With all the grace will soon be past,
  And seen of us no more.

We soon shall bid the whole farewell,
  And pass up once away ;
No more romantic tales to tell,
  Since here we cannot stay.

Those fields all fenceless void of flowers,
  Will soon be left in shame ;
To fade with all the falling showers,
  Whence none its loss reclaimed.

We leave the well without supply,
  The streams forbear to flow ;
The cooling springs of all run dry,
  With nothing left to grow.

The Queen without a diadem,
    A King without a throne;
Sequestered like Jerusalem,
    When all her trains were gone.

We've wandered thus from place to place,
    On life's precarious way:
Until you run lifes transient race,
    And camp beyond the grave.

Where'er we lodged, we there must stay,
    Forever hence to dwell;
Hence never to be called away,
    From heaven or from hell.

Still slow, we move from place to place,
    Like bees from flower to flower;
Or faithful saints from grace to grace,
    Move by superior power.

But soon we trust to move our last,
    No more the States to roam;
When the decision will be past.
    And all arrive at home.

LANGUISHING FOR SOME ONE.

Oh! when will the winter be over,
    The cold chilly winds cease to blow;
The fall of my soul to recover,
    Benumbed in these valleys of snow.

My vast Northern distance doth grieve thee,
  The sun from the South shines in vain;
And yields not one beam to relieve me,
  And thus I am left to complain.

No prospect of sweet vegitation,
  Nor news of the blossoms of May;
An object of sad desolation,
  Alone in these valleys I stray.

There's nothing in nature to cheer me,
  Confined in this hibernal chain;
I cry, but no ear seems to hear me,
  An still I am left to complain.

I strive, but I cannot be jolly,
  I try, but I cannot be brave;
Then sink into dull melancholy,
  With nothing in front but the grave.

Death seems resolving to take me,
  Which threatens me often by pain;
And whispers that life will forsake me,
  Thus how can I fail to complain.

Oh mercy! how long shall I shiver,
  And shake in this system of clay;
When will thou my spirit deliver,
  And chase the cold winter away.

When trees are in full bloom of glory,
  The birds strike a wonderful strain;
The dove tells her sweet lovely story,
  And bids me forbear to complain.

Oh! tell me that spring is returning,
   And winter will shortly be o'er;
For then like the lark of the morning,
   My gratified spirit will soar.

Whence once the cold breeze has deserted,
   The soul like the unruffled main,
Is changed or completely converted,
   And ceases at once to complain.

THE UNAWAKENED PENITENT RETURNING FROM THE CAMP.

Fast in bonds I yet remain,
   With fetters on the wing,
Left without one drop of rain;
   To cheer or make me sing,
Heavenly fire now touch the tongue,
   How sinful man by nature dumb;
Humble praise shall then be sung,
   Whilst on our journey home.

Am I sadly left without
   One soul reviving shower,
Sunk beneath the gloom of doubt,
   In this decisive hour;
Heavenly visions fill the eye,
   Of one thus blind by nature's doom,
On the way I pleading lie,
   For light to guide me home.

Lord has Gilead's withdrawn,
  The gospel olive dead!
Has the cloud passed by and gone,
  And left us void of bread?
Tho' we leave the fountain dry,
  The cloud may yet return and come,
Thou art able to supply,
  And fill us Lord, at home.

Many thoughtless souls have gone,
  Like Zacchius up the tree,
Moved by fancy to look on,
  But caught the blaze from thee,
Notwithstanding vast the crowd,
  We see for him there still was room,
Boundless love brings down the proud,
  And peace awaits him home.

See that prodigal brought low,
  To crave the food of swine,
Whose condition was to show,
  The sad effects of wine,
Yet a father's boundless grace,
  Forbids the wretched to roam,
Tho' by sensual pleasures base,
  Is crowned with love at home.

That vile wretch with devils fought,
  Who cut himself with stones,
To himself by love was brought,
  And thus forgot his moans,
There trembling at the voice,
  Which broke with power thro' every tom
Mercy bade the man rejoice,
  And sent him shouting home.

SNAPS FOR DINNER, SNAPS FOR BREAKFAST AND SNAPS FOR SUPPER.

Come into dinner squalls the dame,
   You need it now perhaps,
But hear the husband's loud exclaim,
   I do not like your snaps,
'Tis snaps when at your breakfast meal,
   And snaps when at your spinning wheel,
Too many by a devilish deal,
   For all your words are snaps.

Why do you tarry, tell me why!
   The chamber door she taps,
Eat by yourself, my dear, for I
   Am surfeited with snaps,
For if I cough it is the cry,
   You always snap at supper time,
I'd rather lave in vats of lime,
   Than face you with your snaps.

How gladly would I be a book,
   To your long pocket flaps,
That you my face may read and look,
   And learn the worth of snaps,
I'm sorry that I learning lack,
   To turn you to an almanac,
Next year I'll hang you on the rack,
   And end the date of snaps.

TO THE MUSE.

Dear muse, to thee I lift mine eyes,
   And supplicate thy power;
Tho' at thy feet a suppliant lie,
And heaves his penitential sigh,
   To thy exalted tower.

Gladly I move at thy behest,
   Thou garden of my mind;
Distant from thee I cannot rest,
But where thou art, my heart is blest,
   And all to thee resigned.

Not one that shines among the fair
   Delights me dear like thee,
For when the vapors of despair
Assail my heart, if thou art there
   I crave not else to see.

When lightning blazes o'er my head,
   Thy smiles my ditty form;
The sun of hope beyond the dead,
Why should that soul the thunder dread,
   Or fear to meet the storm.

When mortal life is almost gone,
   Thou beck'nest from the tomb,
The veil will shortly be withdrawn,
The smiles of an ethereal dawn,
   Will swallow nature's gloom.

When fleshly powers decline to sing,
   And love deserts its claim,
My soul tune every dulcet string,
Till my dear muse upon the wing,
   Escorts thee safe away.

THE CLOSE OF LIFE.

To the scene of life now closes.
   Time, farewell to thee;
Oh! that I could die like Moses,
   Drop and strangely flee;
I'm gone, amen—I'm gone forever,
   My eternal debt to pay;
To return again more never,
   Torn from earth away.

Flesh and spirit clept asunder,
   With the flight of breath;
Halt my soul, look down and wonder,
   After gloom of death;
But let no sobbing tones attend it,
   Hide! oh hide! the lifeless frame;
Sobs and tears can never mend it,
   All must die the same.

Man is born not long to tarry,
   A bloom of swift decay;
Death like lightning flies to carry,
   Souls from time away.
His worthless jaw is but a bubble,
   Mortal, what is fortune's crown;
Groping thro' a maze of trouble,
   What is vain renown.

Life is but a cloud of sorrow,
   Oh! but soon to close;
I'm here to-day, but gone to-morrow,
   To my long repose.

See, see, how fast in fates dark ocean,
  Mortals sink beneath the wave;
From a stage of proud devotion,
  Onward to the grave.

Life's dull bush, no spring retrieves it,
  Left without a bloom;
Which, when transient summer leaves it,
  Blossoms for the tomb.
Then, oh my soul, forbear to languish,
  Drop thy mantle on the shore;
Sing, oh death, where is thy anguish,
  Lost and felt no more.

ON EPIPHANY.

Hail wondrous dawn of heavenly grace,
  The Lord is born in Bethlehem;
Gentiles and Jews the King embrace,
  Whose head shall bear the diadem.

With wonder trace, the star of love,
  Which guides the sages of the East;
It seems on silver wheels to move.
  And beckon to a royal feast.

Sing, oh ye heavens, yes souls rejoice,
  To the remotest bounds of earth;
And let creation lift her voice,
  In triumph of the Saviour's birth.

Salvation's planet from the skies,
  Shines forth deliverance to man;
Whilst in a stall the Saviour lies,
  The infant of a glorious plan.

Hark! dont you hear the turtle dove,
   Proclaim thro' the wilderness ;
Give way, ye craggy rocks remove,
   And melt before the sun of peace.

He comes with fire, the wilds to search,
   To bring the stubborn at his feet ;
And to disciplinize the church,
   And render all the law complete.

Fain would I to the manger fly,
   And greet Him with a thousand charms ;
And then like faithful Simeon die,
   With Mary's infant in my arms.

RACHAEL OR VIRTUE.

When I set out a stranger,
I was then a distant ranger ;
The way was blocked with danger,
   I traveled, but the way was never clear,
I fancied the lie, that the world was but a trap,
And I was a fool when I woke from my nap ;
    Take care Molly,
    You make me melancholy,
   I love you much, but Rachael is my dear.

When I began to study,
And found the way still muddy ;
The way for every body,
   Throughout this wide world to steer,
I heard from the vale the sweet counsel of life,
Oh! never leave your studies for the sake of a wife ;
    Take care Fanny,
    Dear little Kate and Annie,
   I love you all, but Rachael is my dear.

Still far though was Rachael's distance,
 And thus I found resistance ;
I found but dull assistance,
   This life is lodged with care.
Lay first a solid base for the comfort of life,
Accumulate your treasure first, and then take a wife ;
     Take care Nancy,
     You well please my fancy,
  I love you well, but Rachael is my dear.

THE SOLDIER'S THOUGHT OF HOME AT THE END OF THE WAR.

The storm arose, but now is past,
   And left behind the calm of joy :
It came, but was not long to last,
   To conquer or destroy.

I never shall in life forget,
   Through future years of time to come ;
And do not now the rout regret,
   Tho' far away from home.

'Tis true, I love the thought of home,
   No less I love to fight a foe ;
Resolved to wear the glorious plume,
   Wherever I may go.

Beware, I love the ladies too,
   And smile on every female bloom ;
Still in the field, I must be true,
   And fight for friends at home.

I love to talk of things long past,
   'Tis both a pleasure and a pain ;
But pleasure is but short to last,
   For time soon breaks its chain.

A FAINT DESCRIPTION FROM THE PLAINS OF MICHIGAN.

Fair princess of the Western shore,
   I smile to look on thee,
'Tis sweet thy wonders to explore,
For such I have not seen before,
   Nor did I think to see,
Thy purling streams meandering clear,
Are music to my silent ear.

Was Eden a more glorious scene,
   In her full bloom,
Or Canaan's land adorned and green,
With every song inspiring plain,
   Entirely void of gloom,
Perhaps they might in wonder shine,
Their grace is nothing more than thine.

When from the rocking boat I gazed,
   On thy bewildering shore,
My tracing eye was much arrayed,
My muse up to her height was raised,
   Those beauties to adore,
What pen can bring the contrast forth,
That lies between the North and South.

Still, still, like Adam when alone,
　　Thus void I must despair,
And heave a melancholy tone,
I cannot live content I own,
　　With all without the fair,
With all the universe beside,
I have no peace without a bride.

I hence must live a man distrest,
　　If of a lady void,
I hence must live and die deprest,
Nor can I permanently rest,
　　However else employed,
My mind from Paradise must roam,
Without a lady love at home.

FROM LEAVING HOME.

I leave thee but I must return,
　　To one beloved so dear,
Alas! I feel a deep concern,
　　That wakes the dormant tear,
Let hope destroy the present pain,
Farewell, till hence we meet again.

I leave thee but I love thee still,
　　Be thou the first and last,
Be my departure where'er it will,
　　Affection holds me fast,
Such fond regard must still remain,
Farewell, till hence we meet again.

I leave thee with a smile and tear,
   It is my fate to move,
However now I disappear,
   Does not dim my love,
I go within affection's chain,
Adieu, till hence we meet again.

LET ME BE THERE.

Let me be there when morn is peeping,
   Loudly with her dripping eyes,
When the world desist from sleeping,
   And the bird mounts in the skies.

Let me be there when noontide breezes,
   Whisper love to all the glade,
And the song the wood lark pleases,
   And the kid plays in the shade.

Let me be there when evening sweetly,
   Spreads her mantle o'er the plain,
When the days close completely,
   And the night comes back again.

Let me be thine and thine forever,
   Whether clad in light and gloom,
Hence to leave thee never, never,
   And thro' life remain to bloom—
        Let me be thine.

A BEAUTIFUL MOONLIGHT NIGHT IN APRIL.

Hail, wonderous queen in ether's vast expanse,
Thy region is immense, and all around
Dim twinkling stars encircle thy bright throne,
And reverence pay to thy superior light,
Thro' fields sublime in smiles of azure pomp;
And fadeless lustre hail thy still approach,
Whilst slow thou com'st on thy silver wheel,
To chase away the fairy midnight gloom,
Robed in the mantle of nocturnal grace.
We view thee lift thy head above the east
To wake the serenade and cities praise,
Arose, the pleasures of the watchful swain,
The boding night bird pours his ceaseless plaint,
Along the breeze shores, the Yadkins fair,
Which, like the extensive Nile imbibes thy song,
Reflected o'er the water as it flows.
Oh! could I gaze from Pilot's lifted mount,
Whilst Phœbe smiles on this delightful eve,
Soft on her bank, that river falls with now,
Inspire my verse with sweet monotony.
And now Aurora on her golden car,
With limpid eyes look forward to the west,
Like some Sultana in her garb of grace,
Mount from her hidden chamber with a smile,
Adorned in saphire glory, lo! she comes,
With rays of splendant breaking from her brow.
The day born herald, Venus, marks her way,
And thus betrays her beauties to the world.
Now Flora, left by Lunar far behind,
She, with delight, reviews her ruined Pan;
And hence, with pleasure starts the morning song,
And wanders humming thro' the woods till noon;
Then with her bosom hung with laurels green,

Deserts the god of shepherds crowned with flowers,
And then imbibes the ventilating breeze.
Thus on her verdant carpet stretched supine,
Traces heaven's blue curtain as she lies
With pensive wonder, while the concave void,
Inspires revolving thought of one supreme.
She next laments Diana's long delay,
And speaks in accents mild to court her charms;
Prolific queen, whilst wilt thou take thy leave,
To dot thy rays on dark Hesperian wilds;
The wanderers of the night would court thy stay
And languish in the absence of thy smile.
Could Joshua, great victor, all divine,
Descend now in the spirit of his faith,
Thy loosened wheel, would at his voice be still,
And thou with sweeter smiles look down from heaven
And bid the nightly song with joy go on.
Now should the prowling wolves disturb the flock,
The shepherd's flute with awe his hunger raged,
The hooting owl would lift his voice in vain,
Wet with the drops of night distilled from heaven;
The stores of vegitation would revive,
From congealation free and void of blast,
The pleasing charms of summer to inspire.
Then could I smile and in my garland's robe,
A visit paid to thy bright festival,
And sporting virgins dance to hear the sound,
So mild and dulcet thro' the pleasant grove,
Till Phebus peeping from his window high,
Throws by the misty curtains of the night
And lifts his torch refulgent up to the east,
Then bids the retinue of Lunar fly,
Pleased with the memory of the late passed night
She bids revolving Phebus haste away.
That meek-eyed Pœhbe may resume her seat.

The pride of ether, and the queen of night,
Whose smiles the rover nymph with tears invoke;
To pay their tribute from the dreary bogs
And sing the memory of a sister's flight.
From fragrant Enna to the shades below
The Whip-poor-will now on the twilight verge
Tracks up her glad exhilarating tone
And Hesper's maids ascends the western States
To light the lamps in the etheral hall.
Like their attendants at some nuptial feast,
Adorned inferior to the bridal queen,
Who leaves her dark abode and slow ascends
Wild up the azure steps the stairs of love.
And stores the upper chambers with superior grace.
Now from the Orient ocean see the bride,
Of hidden Phebus with her silver zone,
With all her glimmering train around her throngs,
And gayed with humble silence on the throne,
She looks a princess or an Eastern bride,
Just from some courtly region of renown,
Arrayed in diamonds or the costly gems,
Which shed their waters on the raptured eye,
Like cytherea on the cradle shell ;
Ascending gently from her native foam,
An infant of affection from her birth,
Too full of beauty not to be admired,
And far too lovely not to be adored ;
And thus Diana soars from earth to heaven,
Whilst Phebus varnishes her silver bowl,
Which like a crystal arch is much delight,
To those who wander through the dreary wilds
At night. Bewildered strangers now may trace,
Her rapid arrows fly throughout the heaven,
And dart with nameless speed to earth below,
Composed of clement rays devoid defeat,

And bids the hidden spectre spring to light,
Thousands of spirits which together meet,
And hand in hand they march beneath their smil
Who slumbering dust lies still in ghostly shades,
Regardless of the melancholy breeze,
And which their dismal voices float along,
Or those which smoothly break from louder gales;
In lyric modulation as from heaven,
'Tis said a minstrel heard them in the night,
Below the moon's pale light they trod there,
And softly breathed a serenade divide,
As winged with grace from Lunar's lucid sphere,
Ethereal concerts seem to move along,
In broken language strangely sweet unknown,
Like harps immortal to revive the sad
With sounds harmonious to the feast of light,
Till lost in awful silence on the minstrel's ear.

ASSASSINATION OF ABRAHAM LINCOLN.

O, cruel fate, too sad to tell,
  Let all the Universe bewail,
  And sob to hear the tragic tale,
And bid the worthy fare-thee-well!
  Arouse ten thousand bitter cries,
  The glory of the country dies!

From State to State the echo flies
  In lamentation for the great,
  The knell of primagenial fate,
He falls, alas! no more to rise!
  The dove still coo's from tree to tree,
  Though he be dead, the land is free!

Still weep, my soul, remain to weep,
  That one so noble thus should die;
  His spirit mount into the sky,
His hallowed bones can only sleep.
  Still, still, the praise to him we give,
  Brave President forever live!

Whoever born must live to die—
  The King, the Regent and the Peer,
  And leave regardless of a tear,
Down trickling from the weeping eye!
  The tears of sorrow may be shed,
  But Lincoln will be never dead!

We never shall forget his name,
  Which must be sculptured in his tomb,
  And flourish in eternal bloom,
The seal of everlasting fame!
  Eternal peer forever soar
  In light, when nature is no more!

MRS. LINCOLN'S LAMENTATION.

What is it for the breezes seem to wail,
The sylvan warblers carol nature's sighs,
For lo! he dies, but leaves behind his name
Eternal Lincoln! weep ye pensive bards,
Loud orators declaim with rills of tears,
For sorrow must attend the dol'rous scene!
Ye damsels of the city weep, O Washington,
Whence is our father fled, gone, gone forever!
Father Abraham the sample of faith,
Whence goest thou to —— ——.

Try the wonders of eternal worlds, but
Still we mourn, but we could not go with thee,
The lady of thy love aspires to thee.
Weep! O my soul, my quick pulse beat thy last,
Ye portals of immortal worlds fly wide,
Eternal messenger go tell my spouse,
To meet me at the threshold of the city,
For lo! I coure in haste from nature's gloom,
Seraphic groups descend and waft me home!
O, Abraham, descend at once and open wide thy b
Ye bright attendant bands escort me hence,
Let me look down on the sulphrous gulf,
And view the rich man with his blistered tongu
The damned, the infernal homicide of peace,
While loud he calls and beckons for relief!
O, father Abraham, send down one drop
Of cooling water to appease the wound,
But ah! too late, the fratrid murderer cries,
My friend, my father Abram, bears me home;
I'm on my way, I'm on my way to heaven.
But oh! the scene is closed and leaves me drear,
Imagination's dream has passed away,
And I awake again, alas! to weep!
Surviving friends, my Abram is no more,
No more to see me till I pass away;
O strike the fatal primagenial blow,
Let me into choas and oblivion
Never more, never, hence to be a woman,
Or thus bereft of all the nature dear!
The lilies droop, the willows sadly weep,
The garden is divested of her grace;
For every scene is pendant as with grief,
And desolation spreads the city around,
The theatre's gloomy where he fell,
With doors and windows closed, where is th

The brave, the glorious, and the friend of man ?
The grave is his asylum, death his friend,
At which from gloom the country rose to light,
On war's last eve the sun of glory sets,
The disk is called in gloom, the star of peace
Break forth in his expanse reflecting glory,
O'er a benighted hemisphere, he leaves
The blaze of day thrown back on every eye.

THE OBSTRUCTIONS OF GENIUS.

I am surveyed by envy's eye,
   By white and colored all the same,
Which oft draws out a secret sigh,
   To feel the ills that bother fame.

Throughout my life I've tried the path,
   Which seemed as leading out of gloom,
Beneath my feet still kindled wrath,
   Genius seemed leading to a tomb.

No cultivating hand was found,
   To urge the night improving slave,
Never by freedom's laurel crowned,
   But pushed through hardship to the grave.

Has philanthropic vigor slept,
   So long in cells of disregard,
While genius in his fetters wept,
   Devoid of favors or reward,

They often fly to trivial pleas,
  To interdict the important cause,
To crush the negligent disease,
  And kill the force of humane laws.

Why did the Gods of Afric sleep,
  Forgetful of their guardian love,
When the white traitors of the deep,
  Betray'd him in the palmy grove.

Let us the evil now forget,
  Which darkened the Columbian shore,
Till sun shall fail to rise and set,
  And slavery's cries are heard no more.

THE BLACK POET.

This work, which is distinct, to be one of the most popular the world has ever known, will be out about the first of October next, and will be offered to the public through agents properly authorized for its sale. Here is a grand opportunity for

ENERGETIC YOUNG MEN,

especially those who have become disabled by the casualties of war, to build up a fortune for themselves. Eminating as it does from the pen of a North Carolina negro,

THE BLACK POET

will be read with admiration and wonder by all. The politician, no matter whether he be for or against the African, will have a curiosity to know what it contains, knowing that the work is backed by such proof as to set forever at rest any doubts that might otherwise arise in the minds of the people as to its being the production of one who has spent his life until a few short months ago in slavery. The philanthropist who inscribes upon his banner

"FREEDOM AND EQUAL RIGHTS TO ALL,"

will certainly want the work, while those whose political training has been such as to teach them that the black man is not capable of being educated, and have therefore no right that white men are in duty bound to respect, will dwell over its pages and rejoice that those whose liberation they are bound to accept as a reality are really possessed of genius, which when properly cultivated will elevate and prepare them to assume the grave responsibilities of that position to which they have lately been called by the proclamation of the lamented Abraham Lincoln.

AGENTS WANTED

IN EVERY TOWN AND COUNTY IN THE UNITED STATES.

Let energetic young men take hold of the matter in good earnest, while the world is discussing the various qualifications of the negro, and they will be more than paid for their trouble.

Send seventy-five cents by mail and

THE NAKED GENIUS,

Second edition, with a circular containing an index of the Black Poet, and the great inducements offered to those who engage in its sale will be sent free of postage.

    Address   WILL. H. S. BANKS,
                        Lawton, Van Buren County,
                                Michigan.

www.ingramcontent.com/pod-product-compliance
Lightning Source LLC
Chambersburg PA
CBHW071241070526
44583CB00017B/2280